The
Dog Department

The Dog Department

James Thurber on Hounds, Scotties, and Talking Poodles

Edited by
Michael J. Rosen

HarperCollins*Publishers*

HarperCollins books may be purchased for educational, business, or sales promotional use. For information please write: Special Markets Department, HarperCollins Publishers, Inc., 10 East 53rd Street, New York, NY 10022.

FIRST EDITION

Designed by Lindgren/Fuller Design

Animation drawings by Mathew Yokom and Bruce Barnes

Printed on acid-free paper

Library of Congress Cataloging-in-Publication Data
Thurber, James, 1894–1961.
    The dog department: James Thurber on hounds, scotties, and talking poodles/James Thurber; Michael J. Rosen [editor].—1st ed.
    p.cm.
    ISBN 0-06-019656-4
        1. Dogs—Fiction. 2. Humorous stories, American. I. Rosen, Michael J., 1954–
    II. Title.
PS3539.H94 D64 2001
813'.52—dc21   00-059789

    02 03 04 05 ❖/RRD 10 9 8 7 6 5 4 3 2

For Sara, Greg, and Mark,
and for Lulu, a German wirehaired pointer,
the newest Thurber great-granddog

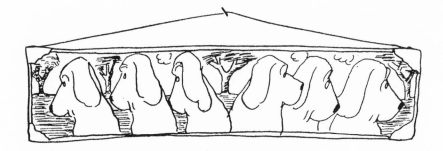

A complete list of accompanying illustrations and cartoons (many of which have not appeared in a book of Thurber's own before) is given on the acknowledgments and sources page at the end of the book. Contributions that appeared as "Talk of the Town" items in The New Yorker *are designated with italics; they are collected here, in book form, for the first time along with three other pieces of prose: "Beaujolais, the Talking Poodle," an unpublished short story; "The Happier Beast," and "Character Readings of our Leading Canines," which concludes the essay "Dogs I Have Scratched."*

CONTENTS

INTRODUCTION

In the spring of 1954 James and Helen Thurber received a letter forwarded by Richard A. Farrar, Creative Designs, in New York City, regarding a complaint from one Mrs. Herbert Shields. The unhappy correspondent had ordered a new scarf decorated with Thurber's art. In Thurber's heyday of drawing, his art was featured on ties, scarves, dresses, and tableware (not to mention in advertisements for products ranging from Talon zippers to Bug-a-boo insecticide, from French Line cruises to Heinz soups). But this customer was clearly disappointed by the nature—or, rather, the *un*nature—of the design, the very Thurber dog itself.

Cheri-Ami Kennels
York Road, Hatboro, Pa.

March 19, 54

Mr. Richard A. Farrar
211 West 12th Street
New York 11, N.Y.

Dear Mr. Farrar:
Enclosed you will find your scarf, and I might add I was rather surprised at the type of scarf it is. I know for a fact I could never

expect someone to pay $3.00 for it. It may be art but it is not a dog. What in heaven's name kind of dog is it supposed to be??

As I explained in my first letter we are a well-known kennel and we are opening a store to sell the type of dog line you would expect to find at a registered kennel. *Only* the pedigree type will do. Now, so I don't bother you any more and so no more of my time is taken up, would you be kind enough to let me know if you do, or do not, have TIES that have heads of pedigreed dogs on? If so you can expect an order from me within the next week. Am enclosing a self-addressed card so you can give me the detailed information.

Sincerely,
Mrs. Herbert Shields

The dog to which Mrs. Shields refers is, of course, that Thurber hound. (Try to discern the exasperated tone of "that *Thurber* hound!" uttered in the same contemptuous manner as a querulous next-door neighbor might have referred to me, at, say, twelve, as "that *Rosen* boy!") Indeed, that Thurber hound has become a creation as elemental and distinctive as Disney's mouse or *Playboy*'s bunny, a creature that embodies something greater than an artist's shorthand for a specific breed; greater, even, than some generic idea of Dog itself. No, the Thurber dog stands for—or sits for, or lies down for—the place of the companion animal in our lives, particularly the canine* presence that waits for us to complete whatever it was we thought so important that it couldn't wait until after a nap, that watches us turn our attention to such fickle amusements as the television or the telephone, that walks beside us as if to convince us that there's no such thing as multitasking, no loftier end to which a walk is supposed to provide a means. Thurber's dog suggests, and silently, too (the way a cartoon suggests with a few lines and few, if any, words, the midst of a situation, allowing us to recognize and to supply the meaning ourselves), the silly, self-conscious, spoiled, and far-flung ways in which we humans

---

*Thurber was not a cat person, and drew very few cats in his kingdom. Cats were not a big part of the Fisher or the Thurber side of his youth, whereas dogs were. His own poor eyesight and eventual blindness made him less comfortable with the startles and surprises included in sharing space with a cat. This fact is hardly lost on his daughter or his granddaughter, Sara, to whom *Thurber's Dogs* is dedicated. They have had many cats in their households, perhaps atoning a bit for their forebear's oversight.

have managed to corrupt or conceal the natural part of our human natures.

Isn't it true, ultimately, that the Thurber dog has the same pedigree as the humans in the picture? We're all the products of someone's imagination.

But why a houndish creature? Thurber grew up with a range of dogs—not one of them any sort of hound. Indeed, the bloodhound as a breed was hardly considered popular—or even very present—in the late 1920s, when Thurber began to doodle his variety. The American Kennel Club records show fewer than seventy registered during those years. Apparently the conformation of the Thurber canine was an unintentional—or "preintentionalist," as he often described his drawings—hybrid. In an interview with *New York Times* journalist Harvey Breit in 1949, Thurber describes the dog's origins as a mistake—rather like the origins of most new breeds: happy accidents.

I had a friend who was on the telephone a great deal and while he talked was always flipping the pages of his memo pad and writing things down. I started to fill up the pad with drawings so he'd have to work to get to a clean page. I began to draw a bloodhound, but he was too big for the page. He had the head and body of a bloodhound; I gave him the short legs of a basset. When I first used him in my drawings, it was as a device for balance: when I had a couch and two people on one side of a picture and a standing lamp on the other, I'd put the dog in the space under the lamp for balance.

I've always loved that dog. Although at first he was a device, I gradually worked him in as a sound creature in a crazy world. He didn't get himself into the spots that human beings get themselves into. Russell Maloney stated once that I believe animals are superior to human beings. I suspected he wanted to get me sore. If I have run down the human species, it was not altogether unintentional. They say that Man is born to the belief that he is superior to the lower animals, and that critical intelligence comes when he realizes that he is more similar than dissimilar.

Extending that theory, it has occurred to me that Man's arrogance and aggression arise from a false feeling of transcendency, and that he will not get anywhere until he realizes, in all humility, that he is just another of God's creatures, less kindly than Dog, possessed of less dignity than Swan, and incapable of becoming as magnificent an angel as Black Panther.

In *The Dog Department* you'll find standard poodles, Scottish terriers, an Airedale terrier, a rough collie, an American Staffordshire terrier—all of which belonged to Thurber family members and many of which have become the subjects of canonical dog tales, such as the story of Muggs, "the dog that bit people," the dog who required James's mother to send her famous chocolates to Muggs's growing list of victims each year.

Here, too, is a fair share about various terriers, bloodhounds, German shepherd dogs, and pugs. But what is remarkable—or comforting, really, since familiarity is one thing we treasure about our life with dogs—is that reading Thurber from seventy-five years ago (the earliest pieces collected here), or those written shortly before his death in 1961, is akin to reading about dogs today; about dogs from the previous century that Thurber must have grown up reading about; about dogs, we hope, from the new century we've just entered. For Thurber, as for all great dog people, there is no hidden life of dogs, only parts of our own lives that we try to bury.

Which isn't to allow that things haven't changed in dog-dom. *If only* we might have had Thurber's take on the new aro-matherapies for stressed out pets, on the rage for VIP ("very important pet") amenity programs at the Four Seasons and other swanky hotels, or on the infrared "watchdog" home protection system, which triggers nothing but a recording of barking dogs when a sensor detects someone in the yard.

Other changes? In Thurber's day our current fancy for retrievers, for example, hadn't begun in earnest. In the 1930s golden and Labrador retrievers were hardly sported in this coun-try, judging from the AKC log of registered animals. Boston ter-riers and Scotties were nearly as popular as cocker spaniels. And today in the United States where those two retrievers rank

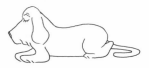

numbers one and two in popularity, Thurber's beloved Scottish terriers have sunk to forty-second place.*

And while we may have the novelty of invisible fences, radio collars, and stricter leash laws, are we any better at ensuring that a dog will obey a command? Isn't the enduring thing about dogs exactly what has endeared them to us: They are beyond our whims and wants, they exceed our pretensions and postures, and, if we take the time to know them, and thus, know ourselves, they eventually reduce us to what Thurber calls, "the happier beast."

Here, then, is James Thurber on all things canine. I'd say "caninonical," if I thought the word would catch on, describing the handful of great writing about dogs that ought to have its own canon. But you get the idea, even if Mrs. Shields didn't:

---

*Just because it's fascinating, our capriciousness with breeds, in 1920, out of 23,454 dogs registered by the American Kennel Club (that's a staggeringly small number, considering that in 1998, roughly that many miniature pinschers alone were registered), the top four dogs were Boston terriers, Airedale terriers, Shepherd Dogs, and collies. The Cocker Spaniel ranked number eleven. One "Retriever" was registered, tying the record for one Scottish Deerhound and one Whippet.

Twelve years later, in 1932, the Cocker Spaniel arrived at the number one position, Boston Terriers continued strong in the number two slot, with Beagles and Smooth-coat Fox Terriers in third and fourth positions. Labs, still low on the list, were on a par with Sealyham Terriers; Goldens were barely outnumbered by Chihuahuas.

Thurber's work has a pedigree all its own. It is dog, quintessentially dog, *and* it is art.

A final word about the selections here. A good portion of material reprinted here comes from *Thurber's Dogs*, which itself gathered many previously published works from Thurber's other books. To this I have added pieces never before collected in book form: drawings and short prose works from *The New Yorker*, and other magazines and books; work that I had the liberty of first collecting in two previous volumes of Thurber's work; and one work-in-progress, the short story "Beaujolais: The Talking Poodle," a story with many drafts that Thurber revised for many years, despite failing to finish it to his satisfaction.

—Michael J. Rosen

Petting

A gentleman who is now at Hatherly Inn, Scituate, Massachusetts, still broods about an incident that happened on Park Avenue when he was here a few weeks ago. His maid had taken his Scottie, named Bunty, out for a walk, and as she was leading him along or he was leading her along—he pulls like the devil—a little girl sitting in a very smart limousine drawn up at the curb cried out, "Oh, please let me pet him!" The maid stooped and was about to lift up the little dog, when the elegant chauffeur of the limousine said, "One moment! Does he bite?" the maid said he didn't. The chauffeur was still worried. "Is he pedigreed?" he asked, doubtfully. The maid said he was. The little girl was then allowed to pet the dog, who asked no questions at all.

JUNE 9, 1934

He lies down on the sidewalk when you're trying to make him heel.

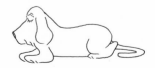

I Like Dogs

I am not a dog lover. A dog lover to me means a dog that is in love with another dog. I am a great admirer of certain dogs, just as I am an admirer of certain men, and I dislike certain dogs as much as I dislike certain men. Mr. Stanley Walker* in his attack on dogs brought out the very sound contention that too much sentimental gush has been said and written about man's love for the dog and the dog's love for man. (This gush, I should say, amounts to about one ten-thousandth of the gush that has been printed and recited about man's love for woman, and vice versa, since Shelley wrote "O, lift me from the grass! I die, I faint, I fail! Let thy love in kisses rain on my lips and eyelids pale.") It is significant that none of the gush about dogs has been said or written by dogs. I once showed a copy of Senator Vest's oration to one of my dogs and he sniffed at it and walked away. No dog has ever gone around quoting any part of it. We see, then, that this first indictment of dogs—that they have called forth so much sentimental woofumpoofum—is purely and

---

*Texas-born Stanley Walker, 1898–1962, worked as a newspaperman for most of his life. He wrote several books, including *The Night Club Era, Mrs. Astor's Horse,* and a biography of Thomas E. Dewey—M. J. R.

I am not a dog lover. A dog lover to me means a dog that is in love with another dog. I am a great admirer of certain dogs, just as I am an admirer of certain men, and I dislike certain dogs as much as I dislike certain men.

simply an indictment of men. I think we will find this to be true of most of Mr. Walker's indictments against the canine world: he takes a swing at dogs and socks men and women in the eye.

Mr. Walker began his onslaught with a one-sided and prejudiced account of how a *little* red chow *on a leash* (the italics are mine) pulled a knife on Mr. Gene Fowler, a large red man who has never been on a leash in his life. Neither the dog nor the woman who was leading the dog are quoted; we don't get their side of the brawl at all. The knife was not even examined for paw prints. Nobody proved anything. There isn't a judge in the world who wouldn't have thrown the case out of court, probably with a sharp reprimand for Mr. Fowler. So far, then, Mr. Walker hasn't got a leg to stand on.

The next crack that Mr. Walker makes is to the effect that the dog is "cousin to the wolf." (He doesn't even say what wolf.) Now, the dog is no more cousin to the wolf than I am niece to the horse. I am aware that until very recently, until this year, in fact, the preponderance of authority has held that the dog *is* cousin to the wolf. But it happens that remarkable and convincing disproof of this old wives' theory has just been adduced by two able and unimpeachable specialists in the field, Charles Quintus Harbison in his *Myths and Legends of the Dog* (Curtis, Webb—$5.00) and D. J. Seiffert in his *The Canidae, a History of Digitigrade Carnivora* (Green & Barton—$3.50). This disposes of this old superstition in a manner that brooks no contradictions. So much for that.

"The history of the dog," Mr. Walker asserts, "is one of greed, double-crossing, and unspeakable lechery." Mr. Walker, who writes with a stub pen, frequently mislays his spectacles, and is inclined to get mixed up now and then, undoubtedly meant to write, "The history of man is one of greed, double-crossing, and unspeakable lechery." If you stopped ten human beings in the street and said to them, "The history of what animal is one of greed, double-crossing, and unspeakable lechery?" seven would say "man," two would walk on hastily without saying anything, and the other would call the police. If you put this same query to ten dogs, none of them would say anything (they are much too fair-minded to go around making a lot of loose charges against men) and none of them would phone the police. (I am reminded to say here, speaking of the police, that no dog has ever held a lantern while a burglar opened a safe belonging to the dog's master. A dog's

paw is so formed that he cannot hold a lantern. If your burglar is smart *he* holds the lantern while the dog opens the safe.)

It is true that now and then a dog will double-cross his master. I have been double-crossed by dogs sixteen or eighteen times; eighteen, I believe. But I find in going back over these instances that in every case the fault really lay with me. Take the time that a Scottish terrier of mine named Jeannie let me down; it is a classic but, I believe, typical example. I was living some eight or nine years ago in a house at Sneden's Landing, on the Hudson. Jeannie and her seven pups lived in a pen in the dining room. It would take too long to explain why. The only other person in the house besides me was an Italian cook named Josephine. I used to come out to the house from New York every night by train, arriving just in time for dinner. One evening, worrying about some impending disaster, or dreaming about some old one, I was carried past my station—all the way to Haverstraw, where I had to wait two hours for a train to take me back. I telephoned Josephine from Haverstraw and told her I would not be able to get there until ten o'clock. She was pretty much put out, but she said she would keep dinner for me. An hour before the train arrived to take me back I got so hungry that I had to eat; I ate several sandwiches and drank two cups of coffee. Naturally when I got home finally and sat down at the dining-room table I had no stomach at all for the wonderful dinner Josephine had kept for me. I ate the soup but I couldn't touch any of the steak. When Josephine set it down before me I said, "Wonderful!" in feigned delight and as soon as she went back into the kitchen I cut it up and fed it to Jeannie. We got away with it fine. Josephine was pleased to see my plate licked clean. It looked as if everything was going to be all right and then Josephine set in front of me the largest piece of apple cake I or anybody else had ever seen. I knew how Josephine prided herself on her cake, but I couldn't eat any part of it. So when she went out to the kitchen for the coffee I handed Jeannie the apple cake, hurried to the door which opened from the dining room into the backyard, and

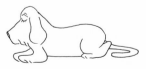

put her out, cake and all. Josephine was in high spirits when she saw with what dispatch and evident relish I had disposed of her pastry. It was while I was in the midst of a long and flowery series of compliments on her marvelously light hand with a cake that there came a scratching at the door. Josephine went over and opened it. In trotted Jeannie still carrying the apple cake.

Now it is my contention (although it wasn't at the time) that I double-crossed Jeannie as much as she double-crossed me. After all, I had filled her with steak (she had already had her dinner) and then asked her to consume an enormous slice of apple cake. She was only about a foot, foot and a half, two feet long, and it was too much for her. I should have known this. But, you will ask, why didn't she bury it, for God's sake? And why, I will ask you right back, should she? Dogs are trained to take and carry whatever you hand them that isn't edible, and they are not supposed to go and hide it somewhere. To Scottish terriers apple cake is not edible. Jeannie had no way of knowing how profoundly she was embarrassing me. A French poodle might have sensed the delicacy of the situation that was bound to develop between me and Josephine if an apple cake which I was supposed to have consumed was carried back into the room by a dog, but a Scottie would never have got the idea. Scotties have barely enough brains to get around (in this they are no worse and no better than men, they are just about the same).

As for Mr. Walker's numerous examples of dogs who have broken up affairs, near affairs, and marriages between men and women, I find in a careful examination of each of his instances that it was never the fault of the dog. In every case the dog was simply there and served as an innocent means of revealing the clumsiness of the man and the shallowness of the woman. Let us examine two or three of Mr. Walker's case histories. (1) A man sits down on a lady's dog and kills it. The lady turns on the man and throws him out of her life. Mr. Walker tells the story as if Lucy (I shall call the dog Lucy) had purposely followed the man around trying to trick him into sitting down on her. As a matter of fact the dog was asleep at the time. Now, the obvious point to be made here is that the man was lucky to get rid of that woman. A husband, or a lover, kills about one fifth of the things he sits down on and if he gets a wife, or a mistress, who raises hell about it, he is going to lead a miserable life. This particular dog, at the sacrifice

of its life, saved this particular man from an especially nasty fate. I am saddened that Mr. Walker worries about the man in this tragic little triangle. I worry about the dog. The woman, and the man, in this case, might have sighed, after Wordsworth, "Lucy's in her grave and O, the difference to me." But I am reminded of a very acute parody of this famous poem in which the parodist altered only one word, the last. He wrote, "Lucy's in her grave and O, the difference to her." That's the way I look at that.

Case history No. 2: Mr. Walker, calling on a lady whom he intended to take to a masquerade ball, got the lady's dog, a French poodle named Lucille, cockeyed on brandy; in his own words, she was "stiff as a plank." The lady came out of the next room, took the situation in at a glance, and refused to go to the ball. Walker left, without taking the poodle with him. Now I submit that to get a poodle drunk and then walk out on her in the very shank of the evening, leaving her to the harsh mercies of a distraught and indignant mistress, is no way for a gentleman to act. A poodle who has had two brandies (they were forced on her, by the way) is just as eager to go out and make a night of it as you and I are. What is more, on her tenth brandy she will prove to be a hell of a

Now I submit that to get a poodle drunk and then walk out on her in the very shank of the evening, leaving her to the harsh mercies of a distraught and indignant mistress, is no way for a gentleman to act.

sight better companion than most men and women any of us know. Another thing: as a man who has raised dozens of French poodles (and was fond of all seventy-two of them) I can say on firsthand authority that poodles do not like brandy; all they like is champagne and they prefer it in a metal bowl. The fact that Lucille drank brandy with a guest simply proves what a fine hostess she was while batting for her mistress who was in the next room. Mr. Walker states at the time of this abortive little drinking bout he was dressed as Sir Walter Raleigh. The poodle would have gone with him anyway; poodles are game for anything.

Case history No. 3: "A man I know," writes Mr. Walker, "was visiting a lady when a police dog bit the cook in the calf. The woman thought it was the man's fault for some reason. . . . Nothing came of that romance, either." A lucky thing, too, since the woman was obviously feebleminded, blaming something that happened in the kitchen on a gentleman who was sitting in her parlor. In setting out to draw a dark picture of dogs, Mr. Walker has succeeded in drawing the gloomiest picture of woman known to the literature of our day. The fact that all of them owned dogs is of no more importance or relevance than the fact that they had

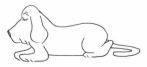

grandfather's clocks or runs in their stockings. A disturbing little group of ladies, if you ask me.

I do not believe in any such sentimentality as that man's best friend is the dog. Man's best friend is man. A friend is one who cleaves to you in spite of the left side of your nature, the dark and sticky side. The dog never sees that side. To him you are one fine guy, without any faults, and that of course is not true and you can't build a friendship on something that is not true. Among the things that every man treasures about his best friends are their weaknesses, the mistakes they have made, the dilemmas they have got into. These afford any friend a great deal of material with which to regale dinner parties or entertain a group of the fellas at a table in a bar. A dog, not recognizing these weaknesses, mistakes, and dilemmas, never tells anyone about them. A great many of the more famous witty remarks made by New Yorkers in the past ten years were made at the expense of some friend. (Example: Mr. W. remarked of his great friend Mr. R., "He is a dishonest Abraham Lincoln.") A dog has no wit.

One time, going through a kennel in Connecticut where people boarded their dogs, I came across a big, handsome, brown

I do not believe in any such sentimentality as that man's best friend is the dog. Man's best friend is man. A friend is one who cleaves to you in spite of the left side of your nature, the dark and sticky side.

water spaniel. He stuck a friendly paw out through the bars of his cage as I walked past, tagged me on the shoulder, and I stopped. I was distressed to discover that he had a huge and ugly swelling on one side of his head. I was surprised that in spite of it he was bright-eyed and gay. Suddenly I found out why. He spit out the swelling. It was a big-league baseball, which he had just been holding in one cheek until someone came along to play with him. He got way back in the far end of the cage—only about eight feet it was—and looked at the ball and then at me. I spent fifteen minutes bouncing it at him. He could catch the swiftest bounces and never missed once. He made Rabbit Maranville* look like a clumsy, fumbling clown. He reminded me of a bull terrier I once had who could catch a baseball thrown as high in the air as you could throw it. I mean you and you and you. A tough guy named Herb Schorey, who could throw a ball as high as any man I have ever seen, lost five bucks betting Rex couldn't catch a ball *he* threw into the air. These are two dogs I have admired.

*Legendary for his clowning antics, infielder Rabbit Maranville (Walter James Vincent Maranville) was a popular figure in baseball from 1912 until 1935—M. J. R.

Rex I liked better than any dog I have ever known and in another place a few years ago I did him some faint, far justice. But I didn't say then and I don't say now that he was the finest and truest and noblest animal that ever lived. The real dog man likes a dog the way he likes a person; the brightest gleam sometimes comes from the flaw. Rex was a gourmand; he twitched and yelped when he slept; he hated Pomeranians and would chew them to bits although he was five times their size; he killed cats; he jumped on horses when they fell down but never tackled one that was on its feet; if you ordered him to stay home he'd slip out the alley gate and meet you five blocks away; he could lick anything this side of Hell and did; he could chin himself with one paw and lift fifty pounds with his jaws; he had a weakness for chocolate ice-cream cones; and although he learned to open the refrigerator door he never learned to close it. The average good dog is that way: I mean the list of his faults would be longer than the sum of his virtues. All in all, Rex was like the men you are fond of—except that when you kill the men they die. Someone beat Rex to death one day but he straight-armed the death angel long enough to wobble home. One of his masters wasn't at the house when he got there (Rex was owned by three brothers), so he stayed alive for three hours by some awful, holy effort that I remember after twenty-five years as clearly as lightning because it was not like anything I have ever seen in the world. When the tardy brother finally arrived home, the dog just managed to touch his hand with his tongue before he dropped dead. Nobody ever more surely earned that long sweet darkness.

If the dog has been ruined for Mr. Walker by fulsome song and silly story, by ornate oration and exaggerated editorial, and by the gibberings of half a dozen ghastly gals, then it has been ruined for him, as I said at the beginning of all this, by men and women and not by dogs.

I have no doubt that the dog can be just as biased and prejudiced as man. I am sure there are some dogs who can't stand men just as there are men who can't stand dogs. I don't see that this proves anything. "I'm always glad," Mr. Fowler said, according to Mr. Walker, "when dogs hate me. It's mutual. When a dog attacks me I know I must be all right."

"When Mr. Fowler attacks *me*," said a prominent dog of my acquaintance recently, "*I* know *I'm* all right. Tell him that when you see him, Mac." I said I would.

Resourceful

A difficult problem was met by a young lady who is a volunteer charity worker when, early this season, she called on an aged and needy couple. She saw at once that their pride would be hurt by the offer of alms of any sort. The samaritan was nonplussed until she saw the couple's dog, an unhappy little wretch of vague descent. "Why, where did you get that dog?" she cried. "I wonder if you realize its value. It's a—a New Mexican setter!"

She then explained that her mother had been searching far and wide for a New Mexican setter and had become a bit cynical about life as the search proved vain. "I would love to surprise her with this dog for her birthday," she went on. "Would you consider parting with it for a hundred dollars?" The bargain was made.

A few weeks later the charity lady returned, and by judicious inquiry found that the old couple's hundred dollars was disappearing. She thought hard. Then her eyes brightened. "Oh, I wanted to tell you," she said. "They won't allow dogs where my mother lives. She wonders if you would mind taking her setter back and boarding him for the winter until the family moves to the country. Mother says she would pay fifteen dollars a week and there's no one she would rather trust him to."

It looks as if the aged couple and their dog would get through the winter, and the young lady has until spring to think up a new idea.

DECEMBER 3, 1927

A Preface to Dogs

As soon as a wife presents her husband with a child, her capacity for worry becomes acuter: she hears more burglars, she smells more things burning, she begins to wonder, at the theater or the dance, whether her husband left his service revolver in the nursery. This goes on for years and years. As the child grows older, the mother's original major fear—that the child was exchanged for some other infant at the hospital—gives way to even more magnificent doubts and suspicions: she suspects that the child is not bright, she doubts that it will be happy, she is sure that it will become mixed up with the wrong sort of people.

This insistence of parents on dedicating their lives to their children is carried on year after year in the face of all that dogs have done, and are doing, to prove how much happier the parent-child relationship can become,

If it can be said that life in any household with any puppy can ever be called a rut.

if managed without sentiment, worry, or dedication. Of course, the theory that dogs have a saner family life than humans is an old one, and it was in order to ascertain whether the notion is pure legend or whether it is based on observable fact that I have for many years made a careful study of the family life of dogs. My conclusions entirely support the theory that dogs have a saner family life than people.

In the first place, the husband leaves on a woodchuck-hunting expedition just as soon as he can, which is very soon, and never comes back. He doesn't write, makes no provision for the care or maintenance of his family, and is not liable to prosecution because he doesn't. The wife doesn't care where he is, never wonders if he is thinking about her, and although she may start at the slightest footstep, doesn't do so because she is hoping against hope that it is Spot. No lady dog has ever been known to set her friends against her husband or put detectives on his trail.

This same lack of sentimentality is carried out in the mother dog's relationship to her young. For six weeks—but only six weeks—she looks after them religiously, feeds them (they

The theory that dogs have a saner family life than humans is an old one, and it was in order to ascertain whether the notion is pure legend or whether it is based on observable fact that I have for many years made a careful study of the family life of dogs. My conclusions entirely support the theory that dogs have a saner family life than people.

At the end of six weeks she tells them to scram.

come clothed), washes their ears, fights off cats, old women, and wasps that come nosing around, makes the bed, and rescues the puppies when they crawl under the floorboards of the barn or get lost in an old boot. She does all these things, however, without fuss, without that loud and elaborate show of solicitude and alarm which a woman displays in rendering some exaggerated service to her child.

At the end of six weeks, the mother dog ceases to lie awake at night harking for ominous sounds; the next morning she snarls at the puppies after breakfast, and routs them all out of the house. "This is forever," she informs them, succinctly. "I have my own life to live, automobiles to chase, grocery boys' shoes to snap at, rabbits to pursue. I can't be washing and feeding a lot of big six-week-old dogs any longer. That phase is definitely over." The family life is thus terminated, and the mother dismisses the children from her mind—frequently as many as eleven at one time— as easily as she did her husband. She is now free to devote herself to her career and to the novel and astonishing things of life.

In the case of one family of dogs that I observed, the mother, a large black dog with long ears and a keen zest for living, tempered

*Owners have too often fixed up fancy quarters for a prospective
mother only to find that she preferred the hall closet.*

only by an immoderate fear of toads and turtles, kicked ten puppies out of the house at the end of six weeks to the day—it was a Monday. Fortunately for my observations, the puppies had no place to go, since they hadn't made any plans, and so they just hung around the barn, now and again trying to patch things up with their mother. She refused, however, to entertain any proposition leading to a resumption of home life, pointing out firmly that she was, by inclination, a chaser of bicycles and a hearth-fire-watcher, both of which activities would be insupportably cluttered up by the presence of ten helpers. The bicycle-chasing field was overcrowded, anyway, she explained, and the hearth-fire-watching field even more so. "We could chase parades together," suggested one of the dogs, but she refused to be touched, snarled, and drove him off.

It is only for a few weeks that the cast-off puppies make overtures to their mother in regard to the reestablishment of a home. At the end of that time, by some natural miracle that I am unable clearly to understand, the puppies suddenly one day don't recognize their mother any more, and she doesn't recognize them. It is as if they had never met, and is a fine idea, giving both parties a clean break and a chance for a fresh start. Once, some

months after this particular family had broken up and the pups had been sold, one of them, named Liza, was brought back to "the old nest" for a visit. The mother dog of course didn't recognize the puppy and promptly bit her in the hip. They were separated, each grumbling something about you never know what kind of dogs you're going to meet. Here was no silly affecting reunion, no sentimental tears, no bitter intimations of neglect or forgetfulness or desertion.

If a pup is not sold or given away, but is brought up in the same household with its mother, the two will fight bitterly, sometimes twenty or thirty times a day, for maybe a month. This is very trying to whoever owns the dogs, particularly if they are sentimentalists who grieve because mother and child don't know each other. The condition finally clears up: the two dogs grow to tolerate each other and, beyond growling a little under their breath about how it takes all kinds of dogs to make up a world, get along fairly well together when their paths cross. I know of one mother dog and her half-grown daughter who sometimes spend the whole day together hunting woodchucks, although they don't speak. Their association is not sentimental, but practical, and is based on the fact that it is safer to hunt woodchucks in pairs than alone. These two dogs start out together in the morning, without a word, and come back together in the evening, when they part without saying good night, whether they have had any luck or not. Avoidance of farewells, which are always stuffy and sometimes painful, is another thing in which it seems to me dogs have better sense than people.

Well, one day, the daughter, a dog about ten months old, seemed, by some prank of nature which again I am unable clearly to understand, for a moment or two to recognize her mother after all those months of oblivion. The two had just started out after a fat woodchuck who lived in the orchard. Something felt wrong with the daughter's ear—a long, floppy ear. "Mother," she said, "I wish you'd look at my ear."

Instantly the other dog bristled and growled. "I'm not your mother," she said, "I'm a woodchuck-hunter."

The daughter grinned. "Well," she said, just to show that there were no hard feelings, "that's not my ear, it's a shortstop's glove."

Litter

Two little boys went into a butcher shop on Lexington Avenue the other Saturday and asked the butcher for dog meat, explaining that their dog had had pups. "How many?" asked the butcher, preparing to wrap up a few scraps. "She has thirty-three," said one of the youngsters. Half a dozen patrons were in the shop, and this threw them into an uproar. The little spokesman for the pair accepted the scraps the butcher gave him (only enough for twelve or fifteen dogs) and walked stiffly to the door, followed by his companion. He turned there, with a look of disgust and disdain for the ignorant persons who had laughed. "She had thirty-four," he said coldly, "but one died."

MAY 20, 1933

A litter of perfectly healthy puppies raised on fried pancakes.

26

How to Name a Dog

Every few months somebody writes me and asks if I will give him a name for his dog. Several of these correspondents in the past year have wanted to know if I would mind the use of my own name for their spaniels. Spaniel owners seem to have the notion that a person could sue for invasion of privacy or defamation of character if his name is applied to a cocker without written permission, and one gentleman even insisted that we conduct our correspondence in the matter through a notary public. I have a way of letting communications of this sort fall behind my roll-top desk, but it has recently occurred to me that this is an act of evasion, if not, indeed, of plain cowardice. I have therefore decided to come straight out with the simple truth that it is as hard for me to think up a name for a dog as it is for anybody else. The idea that I was an expert in the business is probably the outcome of a piece I wrote several years ago, incautiously revealing the fact that I have owned forty or more dogs in my life. This is true, but it is also deceptive. All but five or six of my dogs were disposed of when they were puppies, and I had not gone to the trouble of giving to these impermanent residents of my house any names at all except Hey, You! and Cut That Out! and Let Go!

Names of dogs end up in 176th place in the list of things that amaze and fascinate me. Canine cognomens should be designed to impinge on the ears of the dogs and not to amuse neighbors, tradespeople, and casual visitors. I remember a few dogs from the past with a faint but lingering pleasure: a farm hound named Rain, a roving Airedale named Marco Polo, a female bull terrier known as Stephanie Brody because she liked to jump from moving motor cars and second-story windows, and a Peke called Darien; but that's about all. The only animals whose naming demands concentration, hard work, and ingenuity are the seeing-eye dogs. They have to be given unusual names because passers-by like to call to seeing-eyers—"Here, Sport" or "Yuh, Rags" or "Don't take any wooden nickels, Rin Tin Tin." A blind man's dog with an ordinary name would continually be distracted from its work. A tyro at naming these dogs might make the mistake of picking Durocher or Teeftallow. The former is too much like Rover and the latter could easily sound like "Here, fellow" to a dog.

Speaking of puppies, as I was a while back, I feel that I should warn inexperienced dog owners who have discovered to

> *Canine cognomens should be designed to impinge on the ears of the dogs and not to amuse neighbors, tradespeople, and casual visitors.*

28

their surprise and dismay a dozen puppies in a hall closet or under the floors of the barn, not to give them away. Sell them or keep them, but don't give them away. Sixty percent of persons who are given a dog for nothing bring him back sooner or later and plump him into the reluctant and unprepared lap of his former owner. The people say that they are going to Florida and can't take the dog, or that he doesn't want to go; or they point out that he eats first editions or lace curtains or spinets; or that he doesn't see eye to eye with them in the matter of housebreaking; or that he makes disparaging remarks under his breath about their friends. Anyway, they bring him back and you are stuck with him—and maybe six others. But if you charge ten or even five dollars for pups, the new owners don't dare return them. They are afraid to ask for their money back because they believe you might think they are hard up and need the five or ten dollars. Furthermore, when a mischievous puppy is returned to its former owner it invariably behaves beautifully, and the person who brought it back is likely to be regarded as an imbecile or a dog hater or both.

Names of dogs, to get back to our subject, have a range almost as wide as that of the violin. They run from such plain and

simple names as Spot, Sport, Rex, Brownie and Rover—all originated by small boys—to such effete and fancy appellations as
Prince Rudolph Hertenberg Gratzheim of Darndorf-Putzelhorst,
and Darling Mist o' Love III of Heather-Light-Holyrood—
names originated by adults, all of whom in every other way, I am
told, have made a normal adjustment to life. In addition to the
plain and the fancy categories, there are the Cynical and the Coy.
Cynical names are given by people who do not like dogs too
much. The most popular cynical names during the war were
Mussolini, Tojo, and Adolf. I never have been able to get very far
in my exploration of the minds of people who call their dogs
Mussolini, Tojo, and Adolf, and I suspect the reason is that I am
unable to associate with them long enough to examine what goes
on in their heads. I nod, and I tell them the time of day, if they
ask, and that is all. I never vote for them or ask them to have a
drink. The great Coy category is perhaps the largest. The Coy
people call their pets Bubbles and Boggles and Sparkles and
Twinkles and Doodles and Puffy and Lovums and Sweetums and
Itsy-Bitsy and Betsy-Bye-Bye and Sugarkins. I pass these dog
owners at a dog-trot, wearing a horrible fixed grin.

There is a special subdivision of the Coys that is not quite so awful, but awful enough. These people, whom we will call the Wits, own two dogs, which they name Pitter and Patter, Willy and Nilly, Helter and Skelter, Namby and Pamby, Hugger and Mugger, Hokery and Pokery, and even Wishy and Washy, Ups and Daisy, Fitz and Startz, Fetch and Carrie, and Pro and Connie. Then there is the Cryptic category. These people select names for some private reason or for no reason at all—except perhaps to arouse the visitor's curiosity, so that he will exclaim, "Why in the world do you call your dog *that*?" The Cryptics name their dogs October, Bennett's Aunt, Three Fifteen, Doc Knows, Tuesday, Home Fried, Opus 38, Ask Leslie, and Thanks for the Home Run, Emil. I make it a point simply to pat these unfortunate dogs on the head, ask no questions of their owners, and go about my business.

This article has degenerated into a piece that properly should be entitled "How Not to Name a Dog." I was afraid it would. It seems only fair to make up for this by confessing a few of the names I have given my own dogs, with the considerable help, if not, indeed, the insistence, of their mistress. Most of my

dogs have been females, and they have answered, with apparent gladness, to such names as Jeannie, Tessa, Julie, and Sophie. Sophie is a black French poodle whose kennel name was Christabel, but she never answered to Christabel, which she considers as foolish a name for a dog as Pamela, Jennifer, Clarissa, Jacqueline,

Guinevere, and Shelmerdene. Sophie is opposed, and I am also, to Ida, Cora, Blanche, and Myrtle.

About six years ago, when I was looking for a house to buy in Connecticut, I knocked on the front door of an attractive home whose owner, my real estate agent had told me, wanted to sell it and go back to Iowa to live. The lady agent who escorted me around had informed me that the owner of this place was a man named Stong, but a few minutes after arriving at the house, I was having a drink in the living room with Phil Stong, for it was he. We went out into the yard after a while and I saw Mr. Stong's spaniel. I called to the dog and snapped my fingers but he seemed curiously embarrassed, like his master. "What's his name?" I asked the latter. He was cornered and there was no way out of it. "Thurber," he said, in a small frightened voice. Thurber and I shook hands, and he didn't seem to me any more depressed than any other spaniel I have met. He had, however, the expression of a bachelor on his way to a party he has tried in vain to get out of, and I think it must have been this cast of countenance that had reminded Mr. Stong of the dog I draw. The dog I draw is, to be sure, much larger than a spaniel and not so shaggy, but I confess, though I am not a spaniel man, that there are certain basic resemblances between my dog and all other dogs with long ears and troubled eyes.

The late Hendrik van Loon* was privy to the secret that the dog of my drawings was originally intended to look more like a bloodhound than anything else, but that he turned up by accident with legs too short to be an authentic member of this breed. This flaw was brought about by the fact that the dog was first drawn on a telephone memo pad which was not large enough to accommodate him. Mr. van Loon labored under the unfortunate delusion that an actual bloodhound would fit as unobtrusively into the van Loon living room as the drawn dog does in the pictures. He learned his mistake in a few weeks. He discovered that an actual bloodhound regards a residence as a series of men's rooms and that it is interested only in tracing things. Once, when Mr. van Loon had been wandering around his yard for an hour or more, he called to his bloodhound and

*Dutch-born historian, artist, and humanist Hendrik Willem van Loon (1882–1944), whose books, such as *The Arts* and *Van Loon's Lives,* made him an internationally bestselling author in the twenties and thirties. —M. J. R.

was dismayed when, instead of coming directly to him, the dog proceeded to follow every crisscross of the maze its master had made in wandering about. "That dog didn't care a damn about where I was," Mr. van Loon told me. "All he was interested in was how I got there."

Perhaps I should suggest at least one name for a dog, if only to justify the title of this piece. All right, then, what's the matter with Stong? It's a good name for a dog, short, firm, and effective. I recommend it to all those who have written to me for suggestions and to all those who may be at this very moment turning over in their minds the idea of asking my advice in this difficult and perplexing field of nomenclature.

De Luxe

A gentleman who has lived in five or six world capitals at one time or another and thought he would be thoroughly at his ease anywhere tells us that it took several weeks for him to settle down and relax in an apartment he rented in London Terrace, that modern apartment house which covers a block in new (formerly old) Chelsea. It's his doorman and assistant doorman that well-nigh intimidated him. He'd been there a week when, as he entered one evening, he was preceded by a small, fat poodle dog. The doorman majestically swept open the front door. The assistant, or inner, doorman then opened the inner door, timing it perfectly, so that the dog didn't have to stop and wait. This doorman then rushed over to still another door in the lobby, circling the poodle, and held it open for the dog. This door revealed a flight of steps up which the poodle, looking neither right nor left, and without even a thank-you, proceeded solemnly. Amid perfect silence from his subordinate, the *chef de corridor* then picked up the house phone and said in a deep yet restrained tone, "Good evening, Madam. Theodore is on his way up."

It wasn't three days after this that this same chief doorman had our acquaintance on this same telephone.

"Good morning," he said to the new tenant.

"The what?" said the new tenant.

"The Sanitary Engineer," repeated the doorman.

In the end the functionary was beaten down to the admission that it was the plumber, calling in the matter of a leaking tap.

APRIL 29, 1933

From "The Pet Department"

The idea for the department was suggested by the daily pet column in the New York Evening Post, and by several others.

Q. I enclose a sketch of the way my dog, William, has been lying for two days now. I think there must be something wrong with him. Can you tell me how to get him out of this?

Mrs. L. L. G.

A. I should judge from the drawing that William is in a trance. Trance states, however, are rare with dogs. It may just be ecstasy. If at the end of another twenty-four hours he doesn't seem to be getting anywhere, I should give him up. The position of the ears leads me to believe that he may be enjoying himself in a quiet way, but the tail is somewhat alarming.

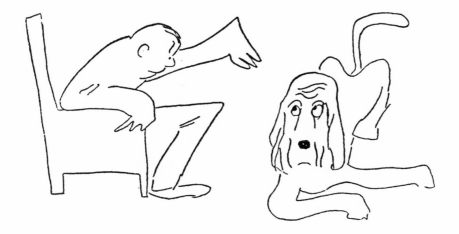

Q. My husband, who is an amateur hypnotizer, keeps trying to get our bloodhound under his control. I contend that this is not doing the dog any good. So far he has not yielded to my husband's influence, but I am afraid that if he once got under, we couldn't get him out of it.

A. A. T.

A. Dogs are usually left cold by all phases of psychology, mental telepathy, and the like. Attempts to hypnotize this particular breed, however, are likely to be fraught with a definite menace. A bloodhound, if stared at fixedly, is liable to gain the impression that it is under suspicion, being followed, and so on. This upsets a bloodhound's life by completely reversing its whole scheme of behavior.

Q. My police dog has taken to acting very strange, on account of my father coming home from work every night for the past two years and saying to him, "If you're a police dog, where's your badge?", after which he laughs (my father).

Ella R.

A. The constant reiteration of any piece of badinage sometimes has the same effect on present-day neurotic dogs that it has on people. It is dangerous and thoughtless to twit a police dog on his powers, authority, and the like. From the way your dog seems to hide behind tables, large vases, and whatever that thing is that looks like a suitcase, I should imagine that your father has carried this thing far enough—perhaps even too far.

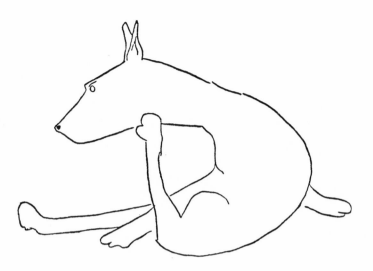

Q. The fact that my dog sits this way so often leads me to believe that something is preying on his mind. He seems always to be studying. Would there be any way of finding out what this is?

Arthur

A. Owing to the artificially complex life led by city dogs of the present day, they tend to lose the simpler systems of intuition which once guided all breeds, and frequently lapse into what comes very close to mental perplexity. I myself have known some very profoundly thoughtful dogs. Usually, however, their problems are not serious and I should judge that your dog has merely mislaid something and wonders where he put it.

Q. No one has been able to tell us what kind of dog we have. I am enclosing a sketch of one of his two postures. He only has two. The other one is the same as this except he faces in the opposite direction.

Mrs. Eugenia Black

A. I think that what you have is a cast-iron lawn dog. The expressionless eye and the rigid pose are characteristic of metal lawn animals. And that certainly is a cast-iron ear. You could, however, remove all doubt by means of a simple test with a hammer and a cold chisel, or an acetylene torch. If the animal chips, or melts, my diagnosis is correct.

Q. Mr. Jennings bought this beast when it was a pup in Montreal for a St. Bernard, but I don't think it is. It's grown enormously and is stubborn about letting you have anything, like the bath towel it has its paws on, and the hat, both of which belong to Mr. Jennings. He got it that bowling ball to play with but it doesn't seem to like it. Mr. Jennings is greatly attached to the creature.

Mrs. Fanny Edwards Jennings

A. What you have is a bear. While it isn't my bear, I should recommend that you dispose of it. As these animals grow older they get more and more adamant about letting you have anything, until finally there might not be anything in the house you could call your own—except possibly the bowling ball. Zoos use bears. Mr. Jennings could visit it.

Q. Sometimes my dog does not seem to know me. I think he must be crazy. He will draw away, or show his fangs, when I approach him.

H. M. Morgan, Jr.

A. So would I, and I'm not crazy. If you creep up on your dog the way you indicate in the drawing, I can understand his viewpoint. Put your shirt in and straighten up; you look as if you had never seen a dog before, and that is undoubtedly what bothers the animal. These maladjustments can often be worked out by the use of a little common sense.

Q. I have three Scotch terriers which take things out of closets and down from shelves, etc. My veterinarian advised me to gather together all the wreckage, set them down in the midst of it, and say, "Ba-ad Scotties!" This, however, merely seems to give them a kind of pleasure. If I spank one, the other two jump me—playfully, but they jump me.

Mrs. O. S. Proctor

A. To begin with, I question the advisability of having three Scotch terriers. They are bound to get you down. However, it

seems to me that you are needlessly complicating your own problem. The Scotties probably think that you are trying to enter into the spirit of their play. Their inability to comprehend what you are trying to get at will in the end make them melancholy, and you and the dogs will begin to drift farther and farther apart. I'd deal with each terrier, and each object, separately, beginning with the telephone, the disconnection of which must inconvenience you sorely.

Don't Move

Y ou've probably heard about the dogs that work for the state police for they get publicity now and then, but Pup, Rex, Nogi, Boots, Skipper, Kim, Nero, and Peggy go pretty much unsung. So would you, no doubt, if you were relegated to Flatbush. That's where these eight German shepherd dogs trot their beats for the New York City Police Department. We went over to find out about them and their work the other day. They are kenneled next to the Police Remount Depot, Ocean Parkway and Avenue W, in Brooklyn, where Sergeant John Healey told us all about his squad of flatpaws. In Commissioner Enright's day, the Department had lots of dogs, but an epidemic carried off most of them. The eight now in service were all presented to the city at one time or another by citizens. As to age, the roll call is: Pup, 10; Rex, 10; Nogi, 9; Boots, 8; Skipper, 6; Kim, 5; Nero, 4; and Peggy, the only bitch, also 4.

Each dog has his own patrolman to work with. Thus Rex's partner is Tom McCabe; Pup's, Daniel Donovan; Nogi's, Jacob Dorer; etc. Man and dog were, in each case, matched with great care, Sergeant Healey told us, the idea being to team up a man and a dog whose natures were as opposite as possible. It seemed

Comb the woods!

somewhat mystical, but we gathered that the Department doesn't want dog and man to become too great pals. None of the patrolmen feeds or grooms his dog (this is done by two officers who never go out with the animals). "These dogs don't regard any man as their friend," Healey told us. "The only man they obey is the patrolman they work with, and they ain't none too polite to him."

Whereupon he sent for one of the dogs, the four-year-old Nero, who came in with his patrolman, Michael Mulcar. Nero, an active, handsome, glossy animal, wore his full equipment: collar, leash, and large leather muzzle with a broad, hard end. "They knock guys down with that muzzle," said Healey, "if they try to get away." Nero walked over and sniffed us. "Hello, doggie," we said. Nero growled. "Don't move," said Healey. We didn't even speak. Mulcare commanded the dog to lie down, and he did. Then he was led away. "You can move now," said Healey.

Each dog patrols a night beat in Flatbush with his officer. The patrolmen stay on the streets but, at the command "Search," the dogs go down dark alleys, into areaways, and over fences into the lawns of private houses, sniffing around for intruders. If a dog finds a man—whether burglar, householder, swain throwing pebbles at a nursemaid's window, or whoever—he stands bristling beside him growling loudly and ominously till the patrolman comes up. The dog never attacks unless the man runs—or pulls a gun. If he runs, the dog dashes between his legs and trips him, or makes a flying tackle at the small of his back and knocks him down. If he pulls a gun, the dog attacks even more viciously, knocking the man down, working up to his gun hand, and with claws and muzzle, disarming him. Gunfire merely infuriates the dog. Both Pup and Boots have been fired at in the past two years. "A shot right in

the face means nothing to 'em," said Healey, proudly. "They're regular members of the Department." Pup and Boots both disarmed their men and were unhurt—a flying police dog is hard to hit.

The dogs practice each day, going up ladders, climbing walls, getting into windows. Now and then at Police Department graduations—and at the Westminster Show—they put on exhibitions. They've been awarded lots of cups and medals, which are kept at the Police Academy. "We don't go in for that," said Sergeant Healey, disdainfully. He likes a real job, not an exhibition. Two years ago Rex, investigating a house closed for the season, grew suspicious of an open window on the back porch and went in to look around. When his growls and snarls brought Tom McCabe, Rex had two thieves cornered in an upstairs room, who were only too glad to surrender to a cop. Now and then a Flatbush burgher or his servant has been cornered by one of the dogs, but the residents of the region know about the dogs and usually stand still till the cop comes up and calls off his partner, and apologizes. The dogs never act sorry. Apparently men are all intruders to them.

SEPTEMBER 19, 1936

Dogs I Have Scratched

There are only a few facts that can be set down as true of all dogs: they are loyal, they are faithful, they are forgiving. Any other generalization is likely to get you into trouble. If you should say that police dogs are trustworthy guardians of little children, some goldfish-and-parrot lady is likely to come forward with a middle-aged wives' tale about a police dog that turned on a youngster and tore him to pieces. Someone else will then cite instances where youngsters have turned on police dogs and torn them to pieces. If it should be said that dogs lie mournfully on the graves of their masters, somebody will recall a cocker spaniel that was too scared of cemeteries to lie on his master's grave. Ardent spanielists will then loudly contend that the spaniel did not know where his master's grave was. This is silly. He did know where it was. I happen to know he knew where it was. He was too scared to go there. I'm not blaming him; I wouldn't lie on anybody's grave even in the warmest kind of weather. This could hardly be called cowardice.

After all, the line between description and cowardice, intelligence and foolhardiness, instinct and reason is fine, and is drawn by some people here and by others there. A cocker spaniel

that attacked an Airedale would be hailed by some as valorous, by others as plain crazy. Cockers are usually fat and short of breath and should go in for gym work and bag punching before taking on the sturdier terriers. But then, that's just my personal opinion. Some would contend that the Airedale would get fat and short of breath before fighting back at a spaniel. I don't know. My point is simply this, however: it is not safe to generalize about dogs. They are as varied as people; lots of them are more varied.

The reason that dogs did not get the upper hand in the misty morning of Time and become the Highest Animal has been explained by Clarence Day in his scholarly treatise *This Simian World*. The dog, loving the slowly evolving supersimian, became his willing slave and lost interest in his own ambitions. I suppose it would be stretching a point to suggest that dogs also had other reasons for not wanting to wrest the power from the apes—that they foresaw, perhaps, how supremacy over the other animals would involve, among other things, riding in the subway, to name but one of the dilemmas that the supermonkey has got himself into.

Dogs may have known that as servants instead of masters they would not be allowed in the White House, or in dentists' chairs, or at the last Yale-Harvard game, which was played in a drenching rain that soaked forty or more thousand people to their superior bones. Dogs would, I am confident, have arranged many things better than we do. They would in all probability have averted the Depression, for they can go through lots tougher things than we and still think it's boom time. They demand very little of their heyday; a kind word is more to them than fame, a soup bone than gold; they are perfectly contented with a warm fire and a good book to chew (preferably an autographed first edition lent by a friend); wine and song they can completely forgo; and they can almost completely forgo women.

Of course it is not strictly accurate to say that the super-simian is supreme and that the dog is his slave. It was true once, but not now. A couple of hundred years ago, the first terriers in Scotland were large rangy beasts but they were so amenable to their masters' wishes that they even grew short legs in order to enter the burrows of the animals their masters were fond of hunting down. This abject state of servitude, this willingness to perform miracles for man, has, I believe, long since ceased to motivate dogs. They are by no means turning over in their minds any idea of getting control—for who would wish to inherit the earth now?—but they have evolved various little systems of their own for running this household and that. I know modern dogs, indeed, who exact a definite servitude of their masters, who even call upon them to perform some of the cruder miracles.

One instance will serve. A small black dog named Tessa had a basketful of puppies in a barn. During a cold and wintry night, the puppies, in the midst of a pillow fight or something of the sort, upset the basket and one of them rolled through a wide crack in the barn floor and disappeared. Not having a flashlight or matches, the puppy got farther and farther under the barn. His mother, unable to get him out, for a dog's paws are not capable of using a crowbar as a lever to pry up boards, simply began to scream peremptorily for her master to get up. And in no obsequious or uncertain terms. Her exact words were "Come on out here!" The master, a spare, nervous man, inclined easily to colds, had been in bed for hours—this was around two o'clock in the morning—but he heeded the commands of his dog and came

Dogs may have known that as servants instead of masters they would not be allowed in the White House, or in dentists' chairs, or at the last Yale-Harvard game, which was played in a drenching rain that soaked forty or more thousand people to their superior bones.

running, in his pajamas, losing one slipper on the way. With the aid of a shovel, he finally dug the puppy out from under the barn, half frozen. (The master, that is, was half frozen: the puppy had all his clothes on and was quite warm.) There are, of course, stories of dogs who have dug men out of tight places, but I don't see what it would prove if I related them. Besides I personally don't know any. I merely suppose there are some.

It is well to bear in mind that the truth about dogs is as elusive as the truth about man. You cannot put your finger on any quality and safely say, "This is doglike," nor on any other quality and say, "This is not." Dogs are individualists. They react to no set bylaws of behaviorism, they are guided by no strict precepts of conduct, they obey unvaryingly no system of instinct, they follow religiously no standard of bloodlines. I know an English bulldog with the manners of a Chesterfield. I know a beagle that can tell time. I know a Scottie that never has the slightest idea what time it is, and I miserably admit to the ownership of a high-bred French poodle that cools its soup by fanning it with a hat.

Character Readings of Our Leading Canines

ROBINSON

He is a deep thinker—that is, he is either a deep thinker or he goes into trances. When the time for action comes, however, he is a dog with all four feet on the ground. Robinson dresses well (in winter), likes to have his food neatly arranged on a plate, and not all mixed up, and he loathes people who call after he has gone to bed. Those who call at godly hours he is civil to, but he never gushes, even though many of his visitors are eminent people in the seven arts. For Robinson belongs to the Dark Lady of the Sonnets. He is a lucky dog.

JACK HOFFMAN

Like all police dogs, he enjoys getting hold of one end of a stick and letting you hold the other end and try to take it away. Many police dogs can throw a sturdy adult at this game, often spraining his back. Hoffman has a certain reputation as a vase breaker, specializing in large Mings. He is an active opponent of cats, which, when he encounters them outdoors, he pursues wildly until they turn on him; he then pretends to be looking for something that he lost. Indoors he confines his unfriendliness for cats

to the making of slighting remarks under his breath. Hoffman often sings late at night when he can't sleep, going in mainly for chants and dirges. He is a father, but has never supported his children.

SANDY

All wire-haired terriers, it has been said, look like champions, and most of them are. For years they have been as good at winning prizes as beagles have been bad at it. (Beagles usually want to lie down when the judges want them to stand up.) Sandy collects sticks, old shoes, belts, small wheels, and anything that can be carried through a door. He knows where most of the missing things in the neighborhood are.

NIGEL

The fact that Nigel, like all Bedlingtons, looks somewhat like a sheep does not mean that he is really like a sheep. He is in every way superior to a sheep, unless you want to make a point of wool. Sheep, after all, are in trade, and the Bedlingtons have always been patricians. Nigel has a quick eye for a menial; even servants dressed in evening clothes don't fool him. He knows one instantly and remembers not to smile or nod. On the other hand he knows a gentleman. If another dog wants to fight, Nigel fights; if the other dog wants to argue, Nigel fights. This gets the matter out of the way, leaving the rest of the day for play and meditation. Bedlingtons are not, however, quarrelsome. They are amiable, but they don't like other dogs. But then what dog does?

BABY

Let not the name of this Pekingese delude you: there is such a thing as a tough baby. Baby looks soft and delicate; lying on a couch she has the appearance of a toy tossed carelessly among the cushions. But she can take her own part, and will, against anything from a Fuller Brush man to a visiting Dauberman-Pinscher [*sic*].

Once, in a brightly lighted speakeasy, an English bull, wearing a tweed cap, leered at Baby and passed some remark. Baby put down her napkin, strolled calmly over to the ruffian, and pulled his cap down over his eyes. "Want any more?" she

asked. He mumbled something about how everyone makes mistakes and that he thought she was some other dog. A burglar in a dark hall would find she was as hard to deal with as a lynx. She tackles low and holds on.

MOE

Moe is one foxhound who lives the life of his master and mistress. At night he sleeps in the same bed with them, in the middle, his head on the pillow; no covers, winter or summer. At first his owners thought this was cute, and they encouraged it. On nights when his master and mistress are out until two or three and sleep until noon, Moe sleeps until noon, too. He has nothing else to do much. Hunting is a practice about which, as a city dog, he knows nothing at all. Bells annoy him because they usually announce people. He would rather sleep than meet the finest people.

INKY

From the windows of his excellent hotel, this cocker spaniel gets an excellent view of midtown Manhattan, which leaves him cold.

His concern is with ground floors and, more particularly, with streets. All the perfumes of Araby could not so entrance him as fifty feet of New York selected at random. His apartment life has made him the faintest bit finicky. He will not eat except out of a specially made bowl, so contrived that his ears hang outside and only his muzzle gets in.

*The dog's attitude toward love remains today
exactly the same as it was in 6000 B.C.*

The Thin Red Leash

It takes courage for a tall thin man to lead a tiny Scotch terrier pup on a smart red leash in our neighborhood, that region bounded roughly (and how!) by Hudson and West Streets, where the Village takes off its Windsor tie and dons its stevedore corduroys. Here men are guys and all dogs are part bull. Here "cute" apartments stand quivering like pioneers on the prairie edge.

The first day that I sallied forth with Black Watch III bounding tinily at the street end of the thin red leash, a cement finisher, one of the crowd that finds an esoteric pleasure in standing on the bleak corner of Hudson and Horatio Streets, sat down on the sidewalk and guffawed. There were hoots and whistles.

It was apparent that the staunch and plucky Scotch terrier breed was, to these uninitiated bulldog-lovers, the same as a Pekingese. But Black Watch must have his airing. So I continued to brave such witticisms as "Hey, fella, where's the rest of it?" and—this from a huge steamfitter—"What d'y' say me an' you an' the dog go somewheres and have tea?"

Once a dockworker demanded, in a tone indicating he would not take Black Watch III for an answer, "What's that thing's name?"

My courage failed me. "Mike," I said, giving the leash a red-blooded jerk and cursing the Scottie. The whole affair was a challenge to my gumption. I had been scared to call my dog by its right name.

The gang was on hand in full force the next evening. One of them snapped enormous calloused fingers at Black Watch and he bounded away, leash and all, from my grasp.

"Black Watch!" I shouted—if you could call it shouting.

"What did y' call that dog, fella?" demanded a man who, I think, blows through truck exhaust whistles to test them.

"Black Watch," said I.

"What's that mean?" he asked menacingly.

"It was a Scottish regiment wiped out at Ypres or some-where," I said, pronouncing it "Eeprr."

"Wiped out where?" he snarled.

"Wiped out at Wipers," I said.

"That's better," he said.

I again realized that I had shown the white feather. That night I took a solemn, if not fervent, oath to tell the next heavy-footed lout that flayed my dog to go to hell. The following evening the gang was more numerous than ever. A gigantic chap lunged forward at us. He had the build of a smokestack-wrecker.

"Psst!" he hissed. Black Watch held his ground.

"They're scrappers, these dogs," I protested amiably.

"What d'they scrap—cockroaches?" asked another man, amid general laughter. I realized that now was the time to die. After all, there are certain slurs that you can't take about your dog—gang or no gang. Just then a monstrous man, evidently a former Hudson Duster who lifts locomotives from track to track when the turntables are out of order, lounged out of a doorway.

"Whadda we got here?" he growled.

"Park Avenoo pooch," sneered one gas-house gangster. The train-lifter eyed Black Watch, who was wagging his tail in a most friendly manner.

"Scotty, ain't it?" asked the train-lifter, producing a sack of scrap tobacco.

"Yeah," I said, as easily as I could.

"Damn fine dogs, Scotties," said the train-lifter. "You gotta good 'un there, when it puts on some age, scout. Hellcats in a fight, too, I mean. Seen one take the tonsils out of a Airedale one day."

"Yeah?" asked the smokestack-wrecker.

"Yeah," said the train-lifter.

"Yeah," said I.

Several huge hands went down to pat a delighted shaggy head. There were no more catcalls or hoots. Black Watch III had been acquitted of Pomeranianism. We're quite good friends now, Black Watch and the gang and I. They call him Blackie. I am grateful to a kind Fate that had given the train-lifter the chance, between carrying locomotives, to see a Scottie in action.

Observations

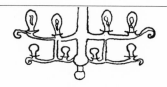

*Secretly they are always comparing you unfavorably
with their former master.*

In time the dog world will undoubtedly have its Freuds and Jungs.

"Here's a study for you, Doctor—he faints!"

Some dogs actually cry.

A dog doesn't necessarily love the person who feeds him.

*If the owner jumps every time he hears the doorbell ring,
the dog will show nervousness too.*

Nor have I found that females are more intelligent than males.

She would show him the way to the safe.

Hors Concours

A rather formidable woman stopped in front of the benches which held the German and French poodles at the dog show last week, and boasted that she had a poodle that could beat all of them. "Why didn't you enter it in the show?" an attaché asked her. "Because I'd have to bring the elephant, too," the woman said. She explained that she owns a traveling animal act and that the elephant mourns if the poodle goes away. Just one of the complications of life.

FEBRUARY 22, 1930

Canines in the Cellar

Belinda Woolf telephoned my mother at the Southern Hotel in Columbus one morning a few years ago and apologized, in a faintly familiar voice, for never having run in to call on her. Something always seemed to turn up, she declared, to keep her from dropping by for a visit, and she was sorry. "I've thought of you, Mrs. Thurber," said Belinda, "I've thought of you every day since I worked for you on Champion Avenue. It's been a long time, hasn't it?" It certainly had. Belinda Woolf was only twenty-three years old when she came to work for us as cook in the spring of 1899, and she was seventy-three when she finally got around to calling her former employer. Exactly half a century had gone by since my mother had heard her voice. Belinda had thought of telephoning for more than eighteen thousand days, but, as she indicated, more than eighteen thousand things had turned up to prevent her.

About a year after Belinda's appearance out of the past, I went to Columbus, and my mother and I drove out to see her. She is now the wife of Joe Barlow, master carpenter of the Neil House, where Charles Dickens used to stay during his western trips a hundred years ago. In fifty years Belinda had not wandered very far. She was living only two blocks from our old house on South Champion Avenue. The weather was warm, and we sat on the veranda and talked about a night in 1899 that we all remembered. It was past midnight, according to an old clock in the attic of my memory, when Belinda suddenly flung open a window of her bedroom and fired two shots from a .32-caliber revolver at the shadowy figure of a man skulking about in our backyard. Belinda's shooting frightened off the prowler and aroused the family. I was five years old, going on six, at the time, and I had thought that only soldiers and policemen were allowed to have guns. From then on I stood in awe, but not in fear, of the lady who kept a revolver under her pillow. "It was a lonesome place, wasn't it?" said Belinda, with a sigh. "Way out there at the end of nowhere." We sat for a while without talking, thinking about the lonesome place at the end of nowhere.

Number 921 South Champion Avenue is just another house now, in a long row of houses, but when we lived there, in 1899 and 1900, it was the last house on the street. Just south of us the avenue dwindled to a wood road that led into a thick grove of oak and walnut trees, long since destroyed by the southward

march of asphalt. Our nearest neighbor on the north was fifty yards away, and across from us was a country meadow that ticked with crickets in the summer-time and turned yellow with goldenrod in the fall. Living on the edge of town, we rarely heard footsteps at night, or carriage wheels, but the darkness, in every season, was deepened by the lonely sound of locomotive whistles. I no longer wonder, as I did when I was six, that Aunt Mary Van York, arriving at dusk for her first visit to us, looked about her disconsolately, and said to my mother, "Why in the world do you want to live in this Godforsaken place, Mary?"

Almost all my memories of the Champion Avenue house have as their focal point the lively figure of my mother. I remember her tugging and hauling at a burning mattress and finally managing to shove it out a bedroom window onto the roof of the front porch, where it smoldered until my father came home from work and doused it with water. When he asked his wife how the mattress happened to catch fire, she told him the peculiar truth (all truths in that house were peculiar) that his youngest son, Robert, had set it on fire with a buggy whip. It seemed he had lighted the lash of the whip in the gas grate of the nursery and applied it to the mattress. I also have a vivid memory of the night my mother was alone in the house with her three small sons and set the oil-splashed bowl of a kerosene lamp on fire, trying to light the wick, and herded all of us out of the house, announcing that it was going to explode. We children waited across the street in high anticipation, but the spilled oil burned itself out and, to our bitter disappointment, the house did not go up like a sky-rocket to scatter colored balloons among the stars. My mother claims that my brother William, who was seven at the time, kept crying, "Try it again, Mama, try it again," but she is a famous hand at ornamenting a tale, and there is no way of telling whether he did or not.

My brightest remembrance of the old house goes back to the confused and noisy second and last visit of Aunt Mary, who had cut her first visit short because she hated our two dogs—Judge, an irritable old pug, and Sampson, a restless water spaniel—and they hated her. She had snarled at them and they had growled at her all during her stay with us, and not even my mother remembers how she persuaded the old lady to come back for a weekend, but she did, and what is more, she cajoled

Aunt Mary into feeding "those dreadful brutes" the evening she arrived.

In preparation for this seemingly simple act of household routine, my mother had spent the afternoon gathering up all the dogs of the neighborhood, in advance of Aunt Mary's appearance, and putting them in the cellar. I had been allowed to go with her on her wonderful forays, and I thought that we were going to keep all the sixteen dogs we rounded up. Such an adventure does not have to have logical point or purpose in the mind of a six-year-old, and I accepted as a remarkable but natural phenomenon my mother's sudden assumption of the stature of Santa Claus.

She did not always let my father in on her elaborate pranks, but he came home that evening to a house heavy with tension and suspense, and she whispered to him the peculiar truth that there were a dozen and a half dogs in the cellar, counting our Judge and Sampson. "What are you up to now, Mame?" he asked her, and she said she just wanted to see Aunt Mary's face when the dogs swarmed up into the kitchen. She could not recall where she had picked up all of the dogs, but I remembered, and still do, that we had imprisoned the Johnsons' Irish terrier, the Eiseles' shepherd, and the Mitchells' fox terrier, among others. "Well, let's get it over with, then," my father said nervously. "I want to eat dinner in peace, if that is possible."

The big moment finally arrived. My mother, full of smiles and insincerity, told Aunt Mary that it would relieve her of a tedious chore—and heaven knows, she added, there were a thousand steps to take in that big house—if the old lady would be good enough to set down a plate of dog food in the kitchen at the head of the cellar stairs and call Judge and Sampson to their supper. Aunt Mary growled and grumbled and consigned all dogs to the fires of hell, but she grudgingly took the plate and carried it to the kitchen, with the Thurber family on her heels. "Heavenly days!" cried Aunt Mary. "Do you make a ceremony out of feeding these brutes?" She put the plate down and reached for the handle of the door.

None of us has ever been able to understand why bedlam hadn't broken loose in the cellar long before this, but it hadn't. The dogs were probably so frightened by their unique predicament that their belligerence had momentarily left them. But when the door opened and they could see the light of freedom and smell the odor of food, they gave tongue like a pack of hunting hounds.

Aunt Mary got the door halfway open and the bodies of three of the largest dogs pushed it the rest of the way. There was a snarling, barking, yelping swirl of yellow and white, black and tan, gray and brindle as the dogs tumbled into the kitchen, skidded on the linoleum, sent the food flying from the plate, and backed Aunt Mary into a corner. "Great God Almighty!" she screamed. "It's a dog factory!" She was only five feet tall, but her counterattack was swift and terrible. Grabbing a broom, she opened the back door and the kitchen windows and began to beat and flail at the army of canines, engaged now in half a dozen separate battles over the scattered food. Dogs flew out the back door and leaped through the windows, but some of them ran upstairs, and three or four others hid under sofas and chairs in the parlor. The indignant snarling and cursing of Judge and Sampson rose above even the laughter of my mother and the delighted squeals of her children. Aunt Mary whammed her way from room to room, driving dogs ahead of her. When the last one had departed and the upset house had been put back in order, my father said to his wife, "Well, Mame, I hope you're satisfied." She was.

Aunt Mary, toward the end of her long life, got the curious notion that it was my father and his sons, and not my mother, who had been responsible for the noisy flux of "all those brutes." Years later, when we visited the old lady on one of her birthdays, she went over the story again, as she always did, touching it up with distortions and magnifications of her own.

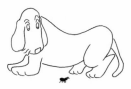

Then she looked at the male Thurbers in slow, rueful turn, sighed deeply, gazed sympathetically at my mother, and said, in her hollowest tone, "Poor Mary!"

My mother's life with animals had been an arduous one since, as a little girl, she had lost a cranky but beloved parrot which had passed some ugly remarks to a big barnyard rooster and got killed for its impudence. She never owned another bird of any kind after that, but as the mother of three sons, and an admirer of dogs in her own right, she was destined to a life partly made up of canine frolic and frenzy. She once told me about a paraphrase of Longfellow that had been spoken to her in a dream: "And the cares that infest the day shall fold their tents like the Airedales and as silently steal away." This must have come to her, of course, during the troublesome period of the Thurbers' life with Muggs, the Airedale that bit people. But Muggs came later, after Rex, and after quite a series of impermanent strays that Mary Thurber's sons lugged home or that naturally found their way to a house containing three boys. One of these was a young German shepherd that we had picked up at a football game and later restored to its lost owners. Another was

My mother's life with animals had been an arduous one since, as a little girl, she had lost a cranky but beloved parrot which had passed some ugly remarks to a big barnyard rooster and got killed for its impudence.

an amiable nondescript that turned up one day from nowhere, spent the week end, and silently stole away after eating my youngest brother's starfish, a dead, dried starfish which Robert kept on a table with a shark's tooth and a trap-door spider's nest, which were left untouched.

My grandfather's collie used to spend as much time at our house as at his own, until the advent of Rex. Both the collie and Rex were demon retrievers, fond of chasing a baseball thrown down the street. One day the collie got to the ball first, only to have Rex snatch it from his mouth and bring it back to us on the

gallop. The two dogs delayed the fight over this incident until that afternoon in the parlor. It was possibly the longest and certainly the noisiest dogfight ever staged in an American parlor, and there were blood and hair and broken Victrola records and torn lace curtains and smashed ashtrays all over the place before we got the battlers separated. The collie, as the aggrieved party, had made the opening slash, and Rex liked nothing better than an opening slash. The long battle ended in a draw and in the departure of the collie for good. He never came back to visit us again.

In later years I set down the brief biographies of both Rex and Muggs, and they appear here in that order.

Insomnia

L atest Ellin Prince Speyer Hospital for Animals story: Two youngsters brought in their dog one evening, woolly and dirty, but busy and waggish. "What seems to be the matter with your dog?" asked an attendant. "He can't sleep," said one of his owners.

APRIL 9, 1932

Your child brings home a scraggly puppy from Lord knows where.

A Snapshot of Rex

I ran across a dim photograph of him the other day, going through some old things. He's been dead about forty years. His name was Rex (my two brothers and I named him when we were in our early teens) and he was a bull terrier. "An

American bull terrier," we used to say, proudly; none of your English bulls. He had one brindle eye that sometimes made him look like a clown and sometimes reminded you of a politician with derby hat and cigar. The rest of him was white except for a brindle saddle that always seemed to be slipping off and a brindle stocking on a hind leg. Nevertheless there was a nobility about him. He was big and muscular and beautifully made. He never lost his dignity even when trying to accomplish the extravagant tasks my brothers and I used to set for him. One of these was the bringing of a ten-foot wooden rail into the yard through the back gate. We would throw it out into the alley and tell him to go get it. Rex was as powerful as a wrestler, and there were not many things that he couldn't manage some-how to get hold of with his great jaws and lift or drag to wherever he wanted to put them, or wherever we wanted them put. He would catch the rail at the balance and lift it clear of the ground and trot with great confidence toward the gate. Of course, since the gate was only four feet wide or so, he couldn't bring the rail in broadside. He found that out when he got a few terrific jolts, but he wouldn't give up. He finally figured out how to do it, by drag-ging the rail, holding on to one end, growling. He got a great, wagging satisfaction out of his work. We used to bet kids who had never seen Rex in action that he could catch a baseball thrown as high as they could throw it. He almost never let us down. Rex could hold a baseball with ease in his mouth, in one cheek, as if it were a chew of tobacco.

He was a tremendous fighter, but he never started fights. I don't believe he liked to get into them, despite the fact that he came from a line of fighters. He never went for another dog's throat but for one of its ears (that teaches a dog a lesson), and he would get his grip, close his eyes, and hold on. He could hold on for hours. His longest fight lasted from dusk until almost pitch-dark,

one Sunday. It was fought on East Main Street in Columbus with a large, snarly nondescript that belonged to a big colored man. When Rex finally got his ear grip, the brief whirlwind of snarling turned to screeching. It was frightening to listen to and to watch. The Negro boldly picked the dogs up somehow and began swinging them around his head, and finally let them fly like a hammer in a hammer throw, but although they landed ten feet away with a great plump, Rex still held on.

The two dogs eventually worked their way to the middle of the car tracks, and after a while two or three streetcars were held up by the fight. A motorman tried to pry Rex's jaws open with a switch rod; somebody lighted a fire and made a torch of a stick and held that to Rex's tail, but he paid no attention. In the end, all the residents and storekeepers in the neighborhood were on hand, shouting this, suggesting that. Rex's joy of battle, when battle was joined, was almost tranquil. He had a kind of pleasant expression during fights, not a vicious one, his eyes closed in what would have seemed to be sleep had it not been for the turmoil of the struggle. The Oak Street Fire Department finally had to be sent for—I don't know why nobody thought of it sooner. Five or

Roy had to throw Rex.

six pieces of apparatus arrived, followed by a battalion chief. A hose was attached and a powerful stream of water was turned on the dogs. Rex held on for several moments more while the torrent buffeted him about like a log in a freshet. He was a hundred yards away from where the fight started when he finally let go.

The story of that Homeric fight got all around town, and some of our relatives looked upon the incident as a blot on the family name. They insisted that we get rid of Rex, but we were very happy with him, and nobody could have made us give him up. We would have left town with him first, along any road there was to go. It would have been different, perhaps, if he had ever started fights, or looked for trouble. But he had a gentle disposition. He never bit a person

in the ten strenuous years that he lived, nor ever growled at anyone except prowlers. He killed cats, that is true, but quickly and neatly and without especial malice, the way men kill certain animals. It was the only thing he did that we could never cure him of doing. He never killed or even chased a squirrel. I don't know why. He had his own philosophy about such things. He never ran barking after wagons or automobiles. He didn't seem to see the idea in pursuing something you couldn't catch, or something you couldn't do anything with, even if you did catch it. A wagon was one of the things he couldn't tug along with his mighty jaws, and he knew it. Wagons, therefore, were not a part of his world.

Swimming was his favorite recreation. The first time he ever saw a body of water (Alum Creek), he trotted nervously along the steep bank for a while, fell to barking wildly, and finally plunged in from a height of eight feet or more. I shall always remember that shining, virgin dive. Then he swam upstream and back just for the pleasure of it, like a man. It was fun to see him battle upstream against a stiff current, struggling and growling every foot of the way. He had as much fun in the water as any person I have known. You didn't have to throw a stick in the water to get him to go in. Of course, he would bring back a stick to you if you did throw one in. He would even have brought back a piano if you had thrown one in.

That reminds me of the night, way after midnight, when he went a-roving in the light of the moon and brought back a small chest of drawers that he had found somewhere—how far from the house nobody ever knew; since it was Rex, it could easily have been half a mile. There were no drawers in the chest when he got it home, and it wasn't a good one—he hadn't taken it out of anybody's house; it was just an old cheap piece that somebody had abandoned on a trash heap. Still, it was something he wanted, probably because it presented a nice problem in transportation. It tested his mettle. We first knew about his achievement when, deep in the night, we heard him trying to get the chest up onto the porch. It sounded as if two or three people were trying to tear the house down. We came downstairs and turned on the porch light. Rex was on the top step trying to pull the thing up, but it had caught somehow and he was just holding his own. I suppose he would have held his own till dawn if we hadn't helped him. The next day we carted the chest miles away

Of course, he would bring back a stick to you if you did throw one in. He would even have brought back a piano if you had thrown one in.

and threw it out. If we had thrown it out in a nearby alley, he would have brought it home again, as a small token of his integrity in such matters. After all, he had been taught to carry heavy wooden objects about, and he was proud of his prowess.

I am glad Rex never saw a trained police dog jump. He was just an amateur jumper himself, but the most daring and tenacious I have ever seen. He would take on any fence we pointed out to him. Six feet was easy for him, and he could do eight by making a tremendous leap and hauling himself over finally by his paws, grunting and straining; but he lived and died without knowing that twelve- and sixteen-foot walls were too much for him. Frequently, after letting him try to go over one for a while, we would have to carry him home. He would never have given up trying.

There was in his world no such thing as the impossible. Even death couldn't beat him down. He died, it is true, but only as one of his admirers said, after "straight-arming the death angel" for more than an hour. Late one afternoon he wandered home, too slowly and too uncertainly to be the Rex that had trotted briskly homeward up our avenue for ten years. I think we all knew when he came through the gate that he was dying. He had apparently taken a terrible beating, probably from the owner of some dog that he had got into a fight with. His head and body were scarred. His heavy collar with the teeth marks of many a battle on it was awry; some of the big brass studs in it were sprung loose from the leather. He licked at our hands and, staggering, fell, but got up again. We could see that he was looking for someone. One of his three masters was not home. He did not get home for an hour. During that hour the bull terrier fought against death as he had fought against the cold, strong current of Alum Creek, as he had fought to climb twelve-foot walls. When the person he was waiting for did come through the gate, whistling, ceasing to whistle, Rex walked a few wabbly paces toward him, touched his hand with his muzzle, and fell down again. This time he didn't get up.

The Dog That Bit People

Probably no one man should have as many dogs in his life as I have had, but there was more pleasure than distress in them for me except in the case of an Airedale named Muggs. He gave me more trouble than all the other fifty-four or -five put together, although my moment of keenest embarrassment was the time a Scotch terrier named Jeannie, who had just had four puppies in the shoe closet of a fourth-floor apartment in New York, had the fifth and last at the corner of—but we shall get around to that later on. Then, too, there was the prize-winning French poodle, a great big black poodle—none of your little, untroublesome white miniatures—who got sick riding in the rumble seat of a car with me on her way to the Greenwich Dog Show. She had a red rubber bib tucked around her throat and, since a rainstorm came up when we were halfway through the Bronx, I had to hold over her a small green umbrella, really more of a parasol. The rain beat

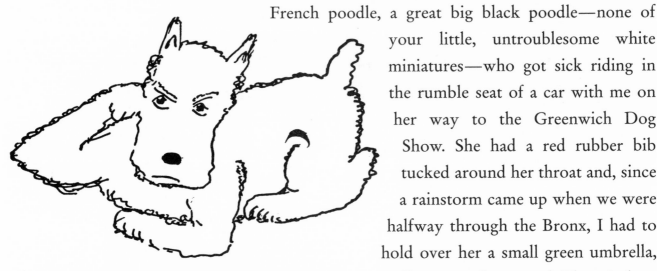

Nobody knew exactly what was the matter with him.

down fearfully, and suddenly the driver of the car drove into a big garage, filled with mechanics. It happened so quickly that I forgot to put the umbrella down, and I shall always remember the look of incredulity that came over the face of the garageman who came over to see what we wanted. "Get a load of this, Mac," he called to someone behind him.

But the Airedale, as I have said, was the worst of all my dogs. He really wasn't my dog, as a matter of fact; I came home from a vacation one summer to find that my brother Robert had bought him while I was away. A big, burly, choleric dog, he always acted as if he thought I wasn't one of the family. There was a slight advantage in being one of the family, for he didn't bite the family as often as he bit strangers. Still, in the years that we had him he bit everybody but Mother, and he made a pass at her once but missed. That was during the month when we suddenly had mice, and Muggs refused to do anything about them. Nobody ever had mice exactly like the mice we had that month. They acted like pet mice, almost like mice somebody had trained. They were so friendly that one night when Mother entertained at dinner the Friraliras, a club she and my father had belonged to

Mother used to send a box of candy every Christmas to the people the Airedale bit. The list finally contained forty or more names.

for twenty years, she put down a lot of little dishes with food in them on the pantry floor so that the mice would be satisfied with that and wouldn't come into the dining room. Muggs stayed out in the pantry with the mice, lying on the floor, growling to himself—not at the mice, but about all the people in the next room that he would have liked to get at. Mother slipped out into the pantry once to see how everything was going. Everything was going fine. It made her so mad to see Muggs lying there, oblivious of the mice—they came running up to her—that she slapped him and he slashed at her but didn't make it. He was sorry immediately, Mother said. He was always sorry, she said, after he bit someone, but we could not understand how she figured this out. He didn't act sorry.

Mother used to send a box of candy every Christmas to the people the Airedale bit. The list finally contained forty or more names. Nobody could understand why we didn't get rid of the dog. I didn't understand it very well myself, but we didn't get rid of him. I think that one or two people tried to poison Muggs—he acted poisoned once in a while—and old Major Moberly fired at him once with his service revolver near the

Seneca Hotel in East Broad Street—but Muggs lived to be almost eleven years old, and even when he could hardly get around, he bit a congressman who had called to see my father on business. My mother had never liked the congressman—she said the signs of his horoscope showed he couldn't be trusted (he was Saturn with the moon in Virgo)—but she sent him a box of candy that Christmas. He sent it right back, probably because he suspected it was trick candy. Mother persuaded herself it was all for the best that the dog had bitten him, even though father lost an important business association because of it. "I wouldn't be associated with such a man," Mother said. "Muggs could read him like a book."

We used to take turns feeding Muggs to be on his good side, but that didn't always work. He was never in a very good humor, even after a meal. Nobody knew exactly what was the matter with him, but whatever it was it made him irascible, especially in the mornings. Robert never felt very well in the morning, either, especially before breakfast, and once when he came downstairs and found that Muggs had moodily chewed up the morning paper he hit him in the face with a grapefruit and then

jumped up on the dining-room table, scattering dishes and silver-ware and spilling the coffee. Muggs's first free leap carried him all the way across the table and into a brass fire screen in front of the gas grate, but he was back on his feet in a moment, and in the end he got Robert and gave him a pretty vicious bite in the leg. Then he was all over it; he never bit anyone more than once at a time. Mother always mentioned that as an argument in his favor; she said he had a quick temper but that he didn't hold a grudge. She was forever defending him. I think she liked him because he wasn't well. "He's not strong," she would say, pityingly, but that was inaccurate; he may not have been well but he was terribly strong.

One time my mother went to the Chittenden Hotel to call on a woman mental healer who was lecturing in Columbus on the subject of "Harmonious Vibrations." She wanted to find out if it was possible to get harmonious vibrations into a dog. "He's a large tan-colored Airedale," Mother explained. The woman said she had never treated a dog, but she advised my mother to hold the thought that he did not bite and would not bite. Mother was holding the thought the very next morning when Muggs got the iceman, but she blamed that slip-up on the iceman. "If you didn't think he would bite you, he wouldn't," Mother told him. He stomped out of the house in a terrible jangle of vibrations.

One morning when Muggs bit me slightly, more or less in passing, I reached down and grabbed his short stumpy tail and hoisted him into the air. It was a foolhardy thing to do and the last time I saw my mother, about six months ago, she said she didn't know what had possessed me. I don't either, except that I was pretty mad. As long as I held the dog off the floor by his tail he couldn't get at me, but he twisted and jerked so, snarling all the time, that I realized I couldn't hold him that way very long. I carried him to the kitchen and flung him onto the floor and shut the door on him just as he crashed against it. But I forgot about the back stairs. Muggs went up the back stairs and down the front stairs and had me cornered in the living room. I managed to get up onto the mantelpiece above the fireplace, but it gave way and came down with a tremendous crash, throwing a large marble clock, several vases, and myself heavily to the floor. Muggs was so alarmed by the racket that when I picked myself up he had disappeared. We couldn't find him anywhere, although we whistled and shouted, until old Mrs. Detweiler called after dinner

that night. Muggs had bitten her once, in the leg, and she came into the living room only after we assured her that Muggs had run away. She had just seated herself when, with a great growling and scratching of claws, Muggs emerged from under a davenport where he had been quietly hiding all the time, and bit her again. Mother examined the bite and put arnica on it and told Mrs. Detweiler that it was only a bruise. "He just bumped you," she said. But Mrs. Detweiler left the house in a nasty state of mind.

Lots of people reported our Airedale to the police, but my father held a municipal office at the time and was on friendly terms with the police. Even so, the cops had been out a couple of times— once when Muggs bit Mrs. Rufus Sturtevant and again when he bit Lieutenant-Governor Malloy—but Mother told them that it hadn't been Muggs's fault but the fault of the people who were bitten. "When he starts for them, they scream," she explained, "and that excites him." The cops suggested that it might be a good idea to tie the dog up, but Mother said that it mortified him to be tied up and that he wouldn't eat when he was tied up.

Muggs at his meals was an unusual sight. Because of the fact that if you reached toward the floor he would bite you, we

usually put his food plate on top of an old kitchen table with a bench alongside the table. Muggs would stand on the bench and eat. I remember that my mother's Uncle Horatio, who boasted that he was the third man up Missionary Ridge, was splutteringly indignant when he found out that we fed the dog on a table because we were afraid to put his plate on the floor. He said he wasn't afraid of any dog that ever lived and that he would put the dog's plate on the floor if we would give it to him. Robert said that if Uncle Horatio had fed Muggs on the ground just before the battle he would have been the first man up Missionary Ridge.

Uncle Horatio was furious. "Bring him in! Bring him in now!" he shouted. "I'll feed the———on the floor!" Robert was all for giving him a chance, but my father wouldn't hear of it. He said that Muggs had already been fed. "I'll feed him again!" bawled Uncle Horatio. We had quite a time quieting him.

In his last year Muggs used to spend practically all of his time outdoors. He didn't like to stay in the house for some reason or other—perhaps it held too many unpleasant memories

for him. Anyway, it was hard to get him to come in, and as a result the garbage man, the iceman, and the laundryman wouldn't come near the house. We had to haul the garbage down to the corner, take the laundry out and bring it back, and meet the iceman a block from home. After this had gone on for some time, we hit on an ingenious arrangement for getting the dog in the house so that we could lock him up

Thunderstorms have driven more than one dog into hysterics.

while the gas meter was read, and so on. Muggs was afraid of only one thing, an electrical storm. Thunder and lightning frightened him out of his senses (I think he thought a storm had broken the day the mantelpiece fell). He would rush into the house and hide under a bed or in a clothes closet. So we fixed up a thunder machine out of a long, narrow piece of sheet iron with a wooden handle on one end. Mother would shake this vigorously when she wanted to get Muggs into the house. It made an

excellent imitation of thunder, but I suppose it was the most roundabout system for running a household that was ever devised. It took a lot out of Mother.

A few months before Muggs died, he got to "seeing things." He would rise slowly from the floor, growling low, and stalk stiff-legged and menacing toward nothing at all. Sometimes the Thing would be just a little to the right or left of a visitor. Once a Fuller Brush salesman got hysterics. Muggs came wandering into the room like Hamlet following his father's ghost. His eyes were fixed on a spot just to the left of the Fuller Brush man, who stood it until Muggs was about three slow, creeping paces from him. Then he shouted. Muggs wavered on past him into the hallway grumbling to himself, but the Fuller man went on shouting. I think Mother had to throw a pan of cold water on him before he stopped. That was the way she used to stop us boys when we got into fights.

Muggs died quite suddenly one night. Mother wanted to bury him in the family lot under a marble stone with some such inscription as "Flights of angels sing thee to thy rest," but we persuaded her it was against the law. In the end we just put up a smooth board above his grave along a lonely road. On the board I wrote with an indelible pencil "Cave Canem." Mother was quite pleased with the simple classic dignity of the old Latin epitaph.

Little Dog

We don't want to embarrass Miss Virginia C. Gildersleeve or her dog, but we feel her "Rules for the Dog's Walkers," as they are officially known, should be told. They might help somebody. She is, as everyone should know, dean of Barnard College and she has a Cairn terrier named Culag. Students are hired to exercise Culag and here are the written rules they must adhere to:

1. The dog is to be exercised for an hour in the morning, generally from ten to eleven. I allow a few minutes leeway at the beginning or the end of the hour, for class purposes, but think he should be out at least fifty minutes. In the afternoon he is to be walked for forty minutes, from 3:00 to 3:40, and then cleaned and brushed for a quarter of an hour.

2. Promptness is absolutely essential. Remember that my household plans often depend upon the dog's departing and arriving exactly at the time fixed.

3. If for any reason you are unable to come, please notify my secretary (University 3200), or my residence (University 4411) as long in advance as possible, so that we can make other arrangements. Do not send a substitute.

4. If I cancel the engagement for any day, I will pay you for the usual time. If you stay away for any reason of your own, however, you do not get paid.

5. I pay at the rate of 50 cents per hour, which I understand to be the usual rate for taking children out. My secretary, Miss Minahan, settles the accounts.

6. Be sure to keep the dog on the lead while on the street, because there is very great danger of his being run over.

7. Please take him down into Riverside Park, and there let him run loose, unless the policeman objects. He needs violent exercise, and you may have to pull him along on the leash to give it to him.

8. He gets exercise in bad weather as well as good. I have a raincoat which I will gladly lend to his walkers.

9. Information for inquirers: Culag is a pedigreed Cairn Terrier, bred in Inverness, Scotland, and his registered name is Culag Boag, which is Gaelic for "little dog."

V. C. Gildersleeve

No freshman need apply, we understand; it takes at least a sophomore to give Culag violent exercise when he doesn't want violent exercise. Both Miss Gildersleeve and Culag interview all applicants. It's probably the way to live.

OCTOBER 13, 1934

And So to Medve

Dog may be man's best friend, but Man is often Dog's severest critic, in spite of his historic protestations of affection and admiration. He calls an unattractive girl a dog, he talks acidly of dogs in the manger, he describes a hard way of life as a dog's life, he observes, cloudily, that this misfortune or that shouldn't happen to a dog, as if most slings and arrows should, and he describes anybody he can't stand as a dirty dog. He notoriously takes the names of the female dog and her male offspring in vain, to denounce blackly members of his own race. In all this disdain and contempt there is a curious streak of envy, akin to what the psychiatrists know as sibling jealousy. Man is troubled by what might be called the Dog Wish, a strange and involved compulsion to be as happy and carefree as a dog, and I hope that some worthy psychiatrist will do a monograph on it one of these days. Even the Romans of two thousand years ago displayed the peculiar human ambivalence about the dog. There are evidences, in history and literature, of the Romans' fondness for the dog, and my invaluable *Cassell's Latin Dictionary* reveals proof of their hostility. Among the meanings of *canis* were these: a malicious, spiteful person; a parasite, a hanger-on. The worst throw in dice

Man is troubled by what might be called the Dog Wish, a strange and involved compulsion to be as happy and carefree as a dog

was also known to the Romans as a dog. Caesar may have been afraid he would throw a dog that day he crossed the Rubicon.

Tracing aspersions on the dog in literature and in common everyday speech is a task for some stronger authority than I, such as the *Oxford English Dictionary*, but there are a few calumnies that I might glance at here, in passing. I remember when "Don't be an Airedale all your life" was a common expression in the Middle West, and a man I knew in Zanesville thirty years ago used the expression a dozen times a day. Shakespeare takes many cracks at Dog from "I would rather be a dog and baying the moon than such a Roman" to "Turn, hellhound!" which Macduff hurls at the bloody Macbeth to start their fifth-act duel with broadswords. The Bard, knowing full well that it is men who are solely responsible for wars, nevertheless wrote, "Cry havoc, and let loose the dogs of war!" But it is not only in the classics that the much-maligned hound has been attacked. A craven pugilist is known to boxing fans as a hound. And I have always resented the words Whittier put in Stonewall Jackson's mouth: "Who touches a hair on yon gray head dies like a dog!" Here it is implied that any soldier who took a free shot at Barbara Frietchie

would be shot, and shooting is rarely the end of a dog. There are a score of birds and animals which could more aptly have been substituted for the dog and I suggest, "Who touches a hair on yon gray head dies like a duck!" But, alas, these ancient libels are past erasing, and Dog will simply have to go on enduring them as patiently as he can.

Stanley Walker, in the old debate of ours that fell so far below the Scopes trial in public interest, condemned the gush that has been written about dogs, as if they and not the female of our own species were the principal object of the sentimental output of men. The truth is that both Dog and Woman have received through the ages undeserved abuse and fulsome praise in about equal measure. But when it comes to the highest praise, for woodwinds, strings, and brasses, Man's favorite theme is the male human being. He describes Woman as a ministering angel, but of himself he cries, "How like a god!"

I wrote somewhere a long time ago that I am not a "dog lover," that to me a dog lover is a dog in love with another dog, and I went on to say that liking or disliking varied, in my case, with the individual dog as with the individual person. Comparing the two breeds as such takes a critic onto sensitive ground, where the climate is changeable and the air is stuffy. A discussion of the relative merits of the ape and the wolf would interest me more than a debate about men and canines. In such a debate the dog could not take part, and when Man began to talk loosely about his Best Friend, or himself, I would reach for my hat and find my way to a neighborhood bar.

Most writers on dogs insist on viewing the animal in a human light, as they insist on teaching it tricks that amuse only humans, and the things people admire most in a dog are their own virtues, strangely magnified and transfigured. A man, to hear him tell it, thinks that lying for several days and nights on a grave is the highest possible expression of loyalty, faithfulness, and devotion, and the finest demonstration of grief. Albert Payson Terhune labored to lift the collie not only above all other dogs in sensitivity and awareness, but seemed to have considered its standards of judgment often superior to those of the human being. He actually believed that his collies stalked out of the room in a show of moral disapproval when whisky was poured into glasses, and never considered the strong probability that the

dogs couldn't stand the fumes of alcohol in their sensitive and aware nostrils, and just walked away. When my mother used to say that Muggs, our mordant Airedale, could read a man like a book, she always implied that the dog was conversant with the fellow's weakness of character. After Muggs had read a man like a book he always growled at him or made his fierce biting leap. In other words, Muggs was a moralist and a reformer, out to punish the weakling and the sinner.

Mother-love, as we call it, the strongest instinct in the female of any species, has always been the most flexible implement in the hands of the sentimentalist. The Scotch collies and the border collies that take part every year in the sheepdog trials in Scotland are hard-working, well-trained, shrewd sheepdogs whose arduous careers have turned them into realists. I have always believed that human fancy adorned one of my favorite Mother-love legends about these collies. The tale tells that a female that had gone out to bark the cattle home was whelped of half a dozen pups, and promptly tucked five of them under a log, picked up the sixth by the scruff of its neck, and came home behind the cows as always, except for the odd, muffled sound of her bark. She then, of course, led her master back to the log. He had sense enough to take a basket, and the pups were brought home in that. My own conviction, after years of meditation about it, is that the collie left all six pups under the log, brought the cows home, and then led her master to where she had hidden the litter. If you have just delivered six pups, you don't have to carry one of them in your mouth to convince a dog owner, even a male dog owner, that a series of blessed events has taken place.

A long time ago, I drove a secondhand Ford sedan up to the Scottish field trials one summer's day. The competition brings together the most experienced sheepdogs of the British Isles. It was won that year, for the second straight time, by an old professional yellow-and-white female with only one eye (maybe she had hidden her puppies under somebody else's log and got a poke in the eye for her intrusion). These dogs have been as carefully educated as bloodhounds or police dogs, and the old-timers go out, bring back six sheep from a distant hill, and put them through all sorts of difficult maneuvers. Each dog is aided only by the whistle signals of his master. Speed and accuracy and smartness of performance count in these sheep-dog trials. The

day I was there, a young male collie, a novice in sheepherding, made his debut, went completely to pieces when his sheep refused to enter a small pen at his bidding, promptly sat down on his haunches, and howled to high heaven. He was disqualified but was cheered by the gallery as his master led him away. But let us get back to America.

One day I heard an anthropologist say that a dog gets whatever conscience it has from its master. The eminent scientist almost stumbled into a familiar trap when he began beating the bushes of this tricky terrain: the assumption that the whole pattern of a dog's behavior, even its own familiar rituals and duties, have to be inculcated in the beast by the Great God Man. Anybody who has observed the behavior of a canine bitch and her litter, from whelping to weaning, knows that this particular piece of human pretension is nonsense. Dogs may have only a sensory, and not a historical, memory, they may have to depend on instinct instead of precept, and their reasoning may lack the advantages of accumulated knowledge, but a female dog knows more about raising her own pups (I except only Jeannie) than any man or woman could teach her. A bitch's discipline is her own, and it lacks the pride, idealism, and dreams of the human female, but it works beautifully and with an admirable economy of effort.

This brings us to Medve (Hungarian for "bear"), my first black standard French poodle, whose posture of repose and thoughtful eyes gave her the appearance of a reflective intellectual, absorbed by the mysterious clockwork ticking behind the outward show of mundane phenomena. Her expression, in these moments of meditation, seemed to be one of compassion, as against the deep contemplative look of the bloodhound, whose sadness, more apparent than real, appears to have grown out of a long consideration of Man's queer habit of becoming lost, stolen, wounded, or crooked. We read most of these thoughts into dogs, as we invent other human qualities for them, but anybody who has known dogs well, and studied them fairly, over a period of fifty years, realizes, without being able to prove it, that not all of their peculiar abilities are invented by human romantics. Medve was a dog who could entertain herself and do without human companionship for long hours on end. She liked to retrieve the apples she found in season under the russet tree, but she had just

Anybody who has known dogs well, and studied them fairly, over a period of fifty years, realizes, without being able to prove it, that not all of their peculiar abilities are invented by human romantics.

121

as much fun throwing an apple herself and chasing it as letting me in on the game. She would pull her head far around to the left, give the apple a quick, hard toss, downhill always, and then chase it and bring it back. She liked to go out into the woods by herself, but what solitary games she may have played there I never found out.

Medve was a professional show dog, who once went Best of Breed at the Westminster Show, but she hated public appearances and was happiest living in the country, where she raised two litters of eleven pups each, seven females and four males both times. She was a professional mother, too. One of the pups of the second litter was continually complaining, in the days immediately following its weaning, that it was sick and had to have milk. Medve would patiently examine the pup with practiced expertness, and, satisfied that it was pretending, push it rudely away with her muzzle. Once, when it became unusually obstreperous, she sent it tumbling over and over. It staggered to its feet, put on a show of limping worthy of a ham actor, and announced, in a kind of squeal I had never heard before, that it had been mortally wounded. Medve went over and picked it up and gave it the careful examination that a squirrel gives a nut, turning it over and over carefully. Satisfied, at last, that it wasn't even hurt, let alone dying, she gave it another, but gentler, shove, and stalked out of its presence and into the house.

She could tell, from thirty yards away, the quality and meaning of her puppies' whimpers, screams, squeals, and protests. When an outcry of any kind began, she would lift her head and listen intently. I never learned to tell the difference between one puppy cry and another, but she knew them all. Often she would saunter out to where the puppies were kept, taking her time; once in a while she would run to them swiftly, like a mother who has got an urgent telephone call, but mostly she would just sigh, put her head on her paws, and go to sleep. She managed the tedium of motherhood with the special grace and dignity of her breed. Scotch Jeannie, on the other hand, went around wearing a martyred look when she had pups to care for, as if she had invented parturition and wished she could turn it off, like a faucet. She responded to every call from the puppy basket with a frown of desperation, and I don't believe she could tell a yip from a yelp, or a yap from a yowl. She was a setup for

the deceitful tactics of her offspring (she didn't even know how to snap an umbilical cord, and usually asked for human help).

Medve, both times, had more puppies than there was room for at table, as one lady writer has put the not uncommon problem, and she didn't know how to take care of this nutritional situation, as smart as she was. I have collected a dozen romantic newspaper clippings on this subject, the most recent this year about a Great Dane bitch who had fourteen pups and not enough dugs to accommodate them. This animal, according to solemn report, developed a command of mathematics and divided the pups into two groups of seven each, so that there were two separate shifts, or servings. If one of the lustier youngsters came back for a second helping, it seems that he was promptly muzzled away. My own experience with dogs has invariably demonstrated the dietary survival of the strongest, and human control is necessary if the weaker pups are not to be undernourished. If Medve couldn't deal with this predicament, then no other dog could. She never rolled on any of her twenty-two pups and crushed them, but this clumsy disaster is common in the case of Great Danes, bloodhounds, and other females of the larger varieties, as it is with tigresses and lionesses in the jungle. There is no sagacious selectivity in it, either, just pure accident. Medve's conscience, in answering or ignoring the commands of her young, was her inherited own, and none of my business, and probably beyond the comprehension of even the most celebrated anthropologists.

In the case of one of her whelpings, the father of the litter kept hanging around, I forget just why, and, in the manner of the male tiger, he began giving the pups boxing lessons when he

thought they were old enough to enjoy rough and tumble. If he got too rough and tumbled one of the pups too far, so that it squeaked, Medve would go for him, with low head and low growl, and nip him on the shoulder and drive him away. The male tiger, incidentally, slips off by himself into the jungle when the female is about to produce cubs, and doesn't return from the bars and the nightclubs until the cubs are fairly well grown, thus avoiding sleepless nights, and annoyance in general. Mother-love, in beasts and birds, can't always be observed carefully, because of innate animal secrecy, but—to revisit an old Ohio highway for a moment—I once encountered a mother quail leading her young across the road in single file. She diverted my attention from them by pretending to have a broken wing, and flopped around almost at my feet, in an exhibition of bravura acting something like that of the late Lionel Barrymore as Rasputin. When the small birds had disappeared into the deep grass, she flew calmly away and joined them. The domesticated dog, to be sure, is accustomed to human interference with its young, and will usually tolerate it patiently. Jeannie was a snapper, though—she once broke the neck of a Siamese cat that approached her puppy basket—and I am glad that it was Medve's litter and not Jeannie's which my two-year-old daughter discovered one day in the barn, and began playing with. Jeannie was as inept in a barn with her young as she was in a shoe closet, and once when she lost a pup under a floorboard she trotted outside and began frantically digging, with one paw, at the base of the stone foundation. I estimated that she would have reached the skeleton of her pup, by that terrier method, in approximately fourteen weeks. (The same thing happened to Tessa, another Scottie of mine, as I have reported somewhere earlier.) The poodle had sense enough to pry up the floorboard in such an emergency, or to ask for help from somebody with muscle and fingers.

A strange phenomenon of family feud, which I was never able to figure out, occurred in the bringing up of Medve's first litter. One of the pups, to me as handsome and genial as any of the others, became an outcast, and its ten siblings continually abused it. In the early weeks Medve always took its part and chastised the attackers, but after they were all weaned she gave the problem no further thought, and I had to drag the culprits away from their victim. The human mother, as I have said before and now

say again, devotes her entire life to her young and to her young's young, a life of continual concern and anguish, full of local and long-distance telephone calls, letters and telegrams, restless nights and worried days, but Medve, like all of her ilk, refused to be bothered after the first few months. She once allowed six of her pups, long past the weaning stage, to take a portable Victrola apart, scatter records all over the place, and chew off, with active and eager teeth, one leg of an upright Ping-Pong table, causing a landslide of paddles and balls, books, ashtrays, and magazines. As long as the grown pups didn't pester Medve, their life was their own, but if she was badgered, she had a unique way of putting the dog in its place, jumping over it gracefully, and giving it a good cuff on the head with one of her hind paws.

Medve's profound dislike of show business caused her to develop a kind of Freudian carsickness, because riding in a car had so often meant a trip to a dog show, as did the long and irritating process of trimming. She was made to wear a red rubber bib, tied around her neck, and a newspaper was always placed on the floor of the car. She threw up on it like a lady, leaning far down, looking as apologetic as she looked sick. At one of the last dog shows in which she was entered with two or three of her best male pups, she was reluctant to get up on the bench assigned to her and her family, and so I got up on it myself, on all fours, to entice her to follow. She was surprised and amused, but not interested, and this was also true of my wife, who kept walking past the bench, saying, out of the corner of her mouth, "Get off that bench, for the love of heaven!" She finally got me off, and the dogs on. The dogs all thought it had been a wonderful interlude, except Medve, who, I am sure, had had a momentary high hope that I was going to take her place in the show.

Medve lived to be fourteen, and after she died I wrote a piece about her called "Memorial" for the newspaper *PM*, which died not long afterward. Of the three of us, I am now the only one left. The brief eulogy, written so soon after my bereavement, has a sunset touch here and there, but I have decided not to let my older and colder hand and mind blur its somewhat dramatic feeling. I know now, and knew then, that no dog is fond of dying, but I have never had a dog that showed a human, jittery fear of death, either. Death, to a dog, is the final unavoidable compulsion, the last ineluctable scent on a fearsome trail, but

Dogs have little sense of time and they are not comforted by tearful good-byes, only by cheerful greetings.

they like to face it alone, going out into the woods, among the leaves, if there are any leaves when their time comes, enduring without sentimental human distraction the Last Loneliness, which they are wise enough to know cannot be shared by anyone. If your dog has to go, he has to go, and it is better to let him go alone. Dogs have little sense of time and they are not comforted by tearful good-byes, only by cheerful greetings. Here, then, with a trace of repetition that I trust will be forgiven, is the piece from *PM*.

Memorial

She came all the way from Illinois by train in a big wooden crate many years ago, a frightened black poodle, not yet a year old. She felt terrible in body and worse in mind. These contraptions that men put on wheels, in contravention of that law of nature which holds that the feet must come in contact with the ground in traveling, dismayed her. She was never able to ride a thousand yards in an automobile without getting sick at her stomach, but she was always apologetic about this frailty, never, as she might well have been, reproachful.

She tried patiently at all times to understand Man's way of life: the rolling of his wheels, the raising of his voice, the ringing

of his bells; his way of searching out with lights the dark protecting corners of the night; his habit of building his beds inside walls, high above the nurturing earth. She refused, with all courtesy, to accept his silly notion that it is better to bear puppies in a place made of machined wood and clean blue cloth than in the dark and warm dirt beneath the oak flooring of the barn.

The poodle was hand in glove with natural phenomena. She raised two litters of puppies, taking them in her stride, the way she took the lightning and the snow. One of these litters, which arrived ahead of schedule, was discovered under the barn floor by a little girl of two. The child gaily displayed on her right forearm the almost invisible and entirely painless marks of teeth which had gently induced her to put down the live black toys she had found and wanted to play with.

The poodle had no vices that I can think of, unless you could count her incurable appetite for the tender tips of the young asparagus in the garden and for the black raspberries when they ripened on the bushes in the orchard. Sometimes, as punishment for her depredations, she walked into bees' nests or got her long shaggy ears tangled in fence wire. She never snarled about the penalties of existence or whimpered about the trials and grotesqueries of life with Man.

She accepted gracefully the indignities of the clipping machine which, in her maiden days, periodically made a clown of her for the dog shows, in accordance with the stupid and unimaginative notion that this most sensitive and dignified of animals is at heart a buffoon. The poodle, which can look as husky as a Briard when left shaggy, is an outdoor dog and can hold its own in the field with the best of the retrievers, including the Labrador.

The poodle won a great many ribbons in her bench days, but she would have traded all her medals for a dish of asparagus. She knew it was show time when the red rubber bib was tied around her neck. That meant a ride in a car to bedlam.

Like the great Gammeyer of Tarkington's *Gentle Julia*, the poodle I knew seemed sometimes about to bridge the mysterious and conceivably narrow gap that separates instinct from reason. She could take part in your gaiety and your sorrow; she trembled to your uncertainties and lifted her head at your assurances. There were times when she seemed to come close to a pitying

comprehension of the whole troubled scene and what lies behind it. If poodles, who walk so easily upon their hind legs, ever do learn the little tricks of speech and reason, I should not be surprised if they made a better job of it than Man, who would seem to be surely but not slowly slipping back to all fours.

The poodle kept her sight, her hearing, and her figure up to her quiet and dignified end. She knew that the Hand was upon her and she accepted it with a grave and unapprehensive resignation. This, her dark intelligent eyes seemed to be trying to tell me, is simply the closing of full circle, this is the flower that grows out of Beginning; this—not to make it too hard for you, friend—is as natural as eating the raspberries and raising the puppies and riding into the rain.

Lady with Dog

This from one who was a member of the Morrow* party on its recent trip from Mexico. The ambassadorial private car was at the front end of the train, between the diner and the baggage car. After lunch, the first day of the voyage home, the porter of a care farther back appeared before Mr. Morrow bearing the petition of a lady who asked permission to pass through the private coach in order to reach the baggage car and feed her dog. Permission was courteously granted, and presently the dog lady barged in with a large bone in one hand. "Pardon me," she said. "It's *so* wonderful to meet the grandparents of our little American prince." The grandparents of the little American prince bowed, the lady went on, and after a time returned, beaming, nodding, murmuring her wonderfuls again. Some time after she had gone back to her car, the porter appeared, looking contrite

*Dwight Morrow, a lawyer, financier, and U.S. ambassador to Mexico at a time of strained diplomatic relations, was the father of Anne Morrow, who married the famous aviator Charles Lindbergh in 1929. Anne and Charles, arguably America's first media celebrities, gave birth to their ill-fated first child, Charles, Jr., in 1930, surely the "little American prince," referred to above. In 1932 the child was kidnapped and murdered. The sensationalism surrounding this, as well as the subsequent Hauptmann trial, was unprecedented. —M. J. R.

and worried. "Mr. Morrow," he said, "I feel you might like to know: I found out that lady ain't got no dog."

NOVEMBER 1, 1930

The Wider World of Dogs

"Shut up, Prince! What's biting you?"

"Other end, Mr. Pemberton."

"Mush!"

"*Are you two looking for trouble, mister?*"

"I'm very sorry, madam, but the one in
the middle is stuffed, poor fellow."

"He's in love with a basset who moved away."

Christabel: Part One

President Truman has revealed a talent for name-calling that would win the admiration of old Andy Jackson, who got shot at in battle, fought half a dozen duels, but would have blanched at the thought of insulting the United States Marines. The president's big slur, for which he so bravely and handsomely apologized later, rang the swords and helmets in the halls of Montezuma and startled the very sands on the shores of Tripoli. And then, while the nation was still buzzing indignantly, Mr. Truman suddenly whizzed his fast ball under the chin of John L. Lewis, declaring that far from making the labor leader ambassador to Moscow, he wouldn't even appoint him dogcatcher.

Now, Mr. Lewis likes nothing better than an exchange of epithets at thirty paces, so he got out his bejeweled dueling pistols and blazed away. As so often happens in these word battles, one of his shots hit an innocent bystander, that old friend of mine, the French poodle. He charged that certain employees of the State Department were "intellectual poodle dogs." The bronze-tongued orator of the coal mines obviously sought to imply by this invidious and gratuitous crack that poodle dogs are intelligent fools.

Now I am a close friend of poodle dogs, having had a lot of them in my time, twenty-five in all, to be exact. I have never known, or even heard of, a bad poodle. Theirs is the most charming of species, including the human, and they happily lack Man's aggression, irritability, quick temper, and wild aim. They have courage, too, and they fight well and fairly when they have to fight. The poodle, moving into battle, lowers its head, attacks swiftly, and finishes the business without idle rhetoric or false innuendo. One spring my French poodle, who was

nine years old at the time, killed three red squirrels in ten seconds, thus saving the lives of hundreds of songbirds, the natural prey of the red marauders. She has never attacked a gray squirrel or a friendly dog, and while she has admittedly engaged in a cold war with cats since 1942, she is too gentle, and too smart, to try to take one apart to find out what makes it purr.

I must confess that many poodles are afraid of lightning, slamming doors, pistol shots, high winds, and things that go

She has never attacked a gray squirrel or a friendly dog, and while she has admittedly engaged in a cold war with cats since 1942, she is too gentle, and too smart, to try to take one apart to find out what makes it purr.

bump in the night, but then so am I. Some of them are high-strung and nervous, but few are neurotic, and they have sensitivity, humor, and dignity. My own poodle is a connoisseur of food one day and a vulgar gourmand the next. She likes rare steak, frogs' legs Provençale, pâté, cheese of any kind, chocolate in any form, and a horrible assortment of things she finds in the fields and woods, old and new, buried and blue. Like most human males, she regards lettuce and the other ingredients of green salads as rabbit food. How any dog who eats a soufflé with dainty and intense enjoyment can leap upon a Milk-Bone or the awful glop called dog candy with equal interest is beyond my understanding. Poodles hate to have their ears monkeyed with or their temperature taken, just as I do, and, like me, they are convinced that creatures who live in holes in the ground must be three times as large as they really are. They are amiable and tolerant, with a healthy prejudice against motorcyclists, tree surgeons, and skiing instructors. They are fond of the butcher, the baker, and the grocer, but hold that the visits of the laundryman and the dry cleaner make no sense and should be discouraged. They make wonderful companions, confidants, and house guests, and are amenable to argument and persuasion. My poodle and I disagree on only two subjects. She contends that my car is a Poodillac and belongs to her and not to me, and that the sound of thunder is made by a four-footed monster the size of a mountain. There is only one flaw in my poodle's honor: she has been known to steal a fried-egg sandwich from me, and then tell my wife that I gave it to her.

A lot of my friends own poodles, among them Charles Addams, the famed connoisseur of ghouls. His poodle's name is Tulip. You want to make anything out of it, Mr. Lewis?

The poodle makes an excellent gun dog and, in the annual American field trials, often wins out over the other retrievers. My own dog was not trained as a retriever and now, at the age of nine, she is convinced that chasing a ball and bringing it back is a futile form of vicious circle, leaving you in the end tired out and just where you were when you started. But she loves to play hide-and-seek, and the day always begins in my house with a foolish attempt on my part to hide from her in one of the eight upstairs rooms. When she finds me—and it usually takes her less than ten seconds—she grins from ear to ear, her eyes twinkle, and she makes the unmistakable sound of laughter. The only time

I ever fooled her was one morning when I called to her and then crawled back in bed. This was against the rules of the game and she was reproachful about it and refused to shake bands with me until late in the afternoon.

The John L. Lewises have gained a distorted notion about poodles because of the unfortunate custom of trimming them in a comic way for dog shows. This deplorable habit of making clowns out of humorists was once thought to go back to the reign of a cruel and playful Roman emperor, but the breed isn't that old. Some of us have hopes that the show trim will be abandoned one day, giving the poodle a chance to establish its true identity and its real nature. In the past twenty years, poodles have become more and more popular in America and have reached the point where they can walk along a street without being jeered at. In 1929, however, a poodle of mine, shown at the Westminster Show in New York, had such little opposition that she won the blue ribbon in her class after having been displayed for only two minutes. The lady who was showing her in the ring was so surprised when the judge gave her dog first prize that she burst into tears. The poodle instantly began to howl, too, in the mistaken belief that their mingled tears were meant to express disapproval of the judge, the bedlam, and the whole distressing spectacle.

The poodle is a freedom-loving dog and does not like to be confined. My present poodle once beat and bit her way through the window of a closed car. Poodles can learn to be seeing-eye dogs in half the time it takes the members of any other breed, but they are rarely used for this purpose because their independent spirit rebels against the repetition of a pattern, because they hate muzzles and leashes, and because they insist on inventing rules of their own. Poodles are great believers in liberty, a thing becoming rare in our day, and they should be allowed to enjoy it.

When my poodle dies, I will bury her sorrowfully under the apple tree, and remember her bright spirit and her gentle gaiety all the years of my life.

Dogs should not make passes at pedestrians.

As You Were

A delighted young lady has told us what she saw from a bus top the other afternoon. On the east side of Fifth Avenue, a middle-aged woman was along with five dogs—two Scotties, a dachshund, a Sealyham, and one unidentified dog. They were scampering around without leashes. When the woman reached the corner of Seventy-second Street, it was apparent that she intended to cross Fifth Avenue, and our young lady wondered how this would be accomplished. Simple. The woman took from her purse a celluloid whistle and blew two sharp blasts on it. The dogs all fell into line, single file, headed by the unidentified dog and brought up in the rear by the dachshund, and, with the woman in the lead, they crossed the Avenue in excellent order. On the other side, the lady blew one long blast, and the dogs fell out again and scampered toward Central Park.

DECEMBER 15, 1934

Christabel: Part Two

My poodle was fourteen years old last May and she is still immensely above ground. She slips more easily than she used to on linoleum, makes strange sounds in her sleep, and sighs a great deal, but more as if she had figured something out than given it up. Her ears are not as sharp as they were, and she often barks at things that aren't there and sleeps through things that are. Her eyes are not much better then mine, but since she can still smell her way around as well as ever, she bumps into fewer things than I do. I have heard whispers, or maybe I just imagine I heard them, that the poodle will live to see *me* laid to rest under the apple tree. When she fell a year ago on the kitchen linoleum and sprained her right shoulder, the veterinarian gave her a couple of shots of cortisone, and she came bounding merrily home from the kennels with the high heart of a schoolgirl on vacation, insisting that our clocks were two hours slow and that it was time for dinner. Someday, long after I am gone, the people who now stop at my front door to ask their way to the Cathedral Pines will want to know if they can show their grandchildren the forty-year-old French poodle.

The poodle's kennel name was Christabel, and she is a *caniche moyen*, or medium-sized French standard poodle. Most people think of all poodles, standard or miniature or toy, black or white or brown, as French, and so did I until a few years ago when I began nosing about in dog books and dictionaries. The poodle actually gets its name from the German word *pud(d)el*, meaning to splash in water, for these dogs, originally German, were used to retrieve wild ducks shot down over lakes. Legend has it that a hunting poodle would swim around all night in a lake hunting for a lost duck, which brings us to an ingenious explanation of the so-called Continental trim of the poodle, familiar to everybody and ridiculous to many. It seems that the back part of the poodle's body was clipped to give it greater agility and speed in the water, that the "bracelets" on the front legs and the pompons or epaulettes near the hip bones were left there to prevent joints from becoming stiff after a long cold patrol of the fowling waters. The tale also tells (most recently in T. H. Tracy's *The Book of the Poodle*) that the pompon on the end of the stubby tail was put there to serve as a kind of periscope by which the hunter could follow the movements of his dog in the water! The exclamation point is mine, because it is surely the front part of the swimming dog that can be most easily

detected, and I am certain that before long somebody will put forward the theory that the red ribbon found in the head hair of some poodles was originally tied there to help the duck hunter locate his circling dog.

Defense counsel for the poodle has his work cut out for him, no matter who makes up the jury he addresses—canine-haters, bassett- or boxer-owners, or lapdog dowagers. The word "poodle" itself is bad enough, but the kennel names of individual members of the breed are worse: Tiddly Winks Thistledown of White Hollow, Twinkle Toes the Third, Little Chief Thunderfoot of Creepaway, and other unlikely compounds of whipped cream and frustrated motherlove, or whatever it may be that causes this sort of thing. The poodle strain caught the fancy some years ago of Park Avenue, Broadway, and Beverly Hills, and these unions have brought about such pet home names as Chi Chi, Frou Frou, Pouf Pouf, Zsa Zsa, and for God's sake don't let me go on like this. The ornamental trim of the poodle, grimly *de rigueur* in dog shows everywhere because it is said to be the best way to exhibit the dog's coat and some of its other show points, has prejudiced people against the great duck retriever for almost five hundred years. (There seems to be no valid evidence of the existence of poodles much earlier than the last half of the fifteenth century, and the tale of the antic Roman emperor who had them clipped to look like lions is, of course, apocryphal.) Whatever the truth may be, the poodle would probably have been laughed out of town and country long ago, had it not been for the sound and attractive clip known as the Dutch trim.

The poodle has been the butt of jokes, all of them pallid as far as I can find out, from Benjamin Disraeli to John L. Lewis, and this had helped to perpetuate the libel that the most sagacious of dogs is an aimless and empty-headed comic. Most apologists, in trying to defend the poodle against this calumny, succeed in making him sound foolisher and foolisher. Very few persons have successfully transcribed the comic talents of a poodle into prose, whether typed or conversational. Something vital and essential dies in the telling of a poodle story. It is like a dim recording of a bad W. C. Fields imitator. My poodle, I am glad to say, does not meet a gentleman caller at the door and take his hat and gloves, or play the piano for guests, or move chessmen about upon a board, or wear glasses and smoke a pipe, or lift the

Very few persons have successfully transcribed the comic talents of a poodle into prose, whether typed or conversational. Something vital and essential dies in the telling of a poodle story. It is like a dim recording of a bad W. C. Fields imitator.

receiver off the phone, or spell out your name in alphabet blocks, or sing "Madelon," or say "Franchot Tone," or give guests their after-dinner coffee cups. She is as smart as any of her breed; indeed she has taken on a special wisdom in what some would estimate to be her seventy-fifth, others her one-hundred-and-fifth year, as human lives are measured, but she has never been trained to do card tricks, or go into dinner on a gentleman's arm, or to say "Beowulf," or even "Ralph." I once tried to get her to ring an old Bermuda carriage bell I picked up years ago, but she was disdainful of this noisy waste of time, and was even more reluctant when I tried to get her to step on the rubber bulb of a 1905 automobile horn. She doesn't like strange unnecessary sounds; she likes quiet and tranquillity.

No, my aged water-splasher has never been taught any tricks that make dinner guests and weekend visitors alert and nervous. If you open the door of your bedroom in the morning, she is not standing there with a newspaper and a glass of orange juice. Somebody once tried to show her how to carry the mail into the house, and she gaily spread the letters all over the front lawn, a lighthearted and sensible way of dealing with my correspondence, which consists largely of invitations to address the Men's Forum of Dismal Seepage, Ohio, requests for something intimate to raffle off at a church bazaar, and peremptory demands, such as: "My sister-in-law has ulcers. Please send her six drawings." The poodle will shake hands, in the gracious manner of her breed, and engage in impromptu house games and lawn games, but she will not appear suddenly at your elbow at the cocktail hour carrying a plate of hors d'oeuvres. She is a country dog, and trembles all over when she is driven in to New York, which isn't often, but the atavistic urge to hunt and swim must have gone out of her bloodline generations ago, leaving no trace. She couldn't tell a mallard or a canvasback from a Plymouth Rock hen, and gunfire appalls her. She can swim a little, but would rather wade. She has never tangled with a skunk or a porcupine, and she has the good sense to beg a woodchuck's pardon if she trespasses on its property, and go back home. When she dances on her hind legs, down near the brook, it means she has discovered a snake, but she would no more close in on one than I would wrassle a bear. She has been known to follow a frog or a toad for hours, with the expression of one who does not

believe her own nose. The rabbits who share my garden produce found out years ago that they could outrun and outzigzag the poodle, and a red fox who lives nearby once trotted right past her, down the driveway and out onto the road, as big as you please. One night the old dog followed a possum up into the woods and didn't come back for two hours. It was my daughter's opinion that the possum had held the poodle for ransom, but finally decided to let her go. This is calumny of a familiar kind and the poodle is used to it. She is not a hunter or a killer, but an interested observer of the life of the lower animals, of which she does not consider herself one. She regards herself as a member of the human race and, as such, she sees no fun or profit in chasing a ball or a stick and bringing it back, time and again. A hundred terriers have made me miserable since before the First World War by laying a ball at my feet and standing there panting and gasping and drooling until I throw it. Nobody my age can throw a baseball as far as I can, because of these long years of practice. I am told that one short-haired fox terrier, for whom I threw a ball all one afternoon, never did come back when I finally wound up and let go. Goody.

In her old age, the Dowager Duchess of West Cornwall has become a touch imperious and has firmly taken her place as a co-equal in the conduct of certain household affairs, particularly those involving meals. She used to lie obediently in the living room, with her paws just over the threshold, but if you are a poodle going on seventy-five or a hundred-and-five, you waive, without consultation, the old rules of behavior. She now removes toast from my grasp if I let my hand fall below what she has established as the point of no return, and now and then she removes from my lap, with a brisk dainty gesture, my napkin, on the ground that the crumbs it has collected belong to her. If you tell her to go in and lie down when you have a dish she especially craves in front of you, she stomps her feet and communicates her flat refusal in a series of guttural sounds very much like an attempt at words. Her range of inflection and intonation, after a decade and a half with people, is remarkable, and I am now able to tell by the quality of her voice, when she is outdoors, who is approaching the house. She not only divides tradespeople into her own classifications, but she has stratified certain friends and acquaintances of ours. Every dog does this, in its minor instinc-

tive way, but without the almost verbal criticism Christabel can bring to her welcome or her inhospitality. She is no longer very hospitable to any caller or visitor, but once a person gets inside the house, she becomes in a flash the perfect hostess, shaking hands, sniffing pockets or purses to see if they contain chocolates or something dug up out of the ground.

She realized, two or three times as quickly as a member of any other breed could have done it, that I had got so that I couldn't see her, and she gets up quietly when I enter a room where she is lying. Once, when I stumbled into her and fell sprawling, she hurriedly examined me from head to foot, with a show of great anxiety, as if she were looking for compound fractures. Christabel regards me as a comedian of sorts, and always knows when I am trying to be funny for her sake, and always smiles (there is no smile quite like a poodle's), and if the joke is a big production number, such as my opening the door to the downstairs lavatory when she asks to be let out, she gives her guttural laugh, turns her head slowly, and lets my wife in on the gag. Now and then she has disapproved of one of my routines and she makes her disapproval unmistakable.

I slipped out of the house one night when she was upstairs, and began hammering on the door. She charged downstairs, barking with the high indignation she had evinced one day when she came upon three tree surgeons who seemed to her to be taking down the maple trees in front of the house. With my coat over my head, I charged into the house, roaring like the late Wallace Beery. With a new sound I had never heard before, she turned and seemed to slither upstairs on her stomach, but she stopped at the landing, deciding to hold that defense until it became untenable. I started up the stairs in a Lon Chaney crawl, and halfway up she recognized me. She didn't think it was funny and wouldn't shake hands for several days.

She likes to be taken to a country restaurant a few miles from home, where she is petted and fed, and which she apparently thinks I own, since she challenges people who arrive for dinner after she has got there. She doesn't like big parties, unless they are composed only of the half-dozen persons she truly admires, and she goes out into the kitchen until the last car has driven away. Not long ago, at a house where there were many people and three or four dogs, she became bored when voices were raised in song,

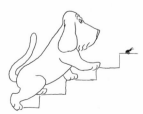

and asked someone to let her out. Half an hour later, the couple that works for us, driving along the road in their car, caught in their headlights a black dog with a yellow collar trotting squarely down the road, and they picked her up. She had come more than a mile from the house of the party she didn't like, and she was on the right road, too, headed for home, but she had a good four miles to go, and that's a long trip for so old a dog. I am confident that she would have got there all right, age or no age.

I said in "Christabel: Part One" something about burying the old poodle under the apple tree. I take it back. I have no doubt now but that she will see me buried first, but she won't lie on my grave for days and nights on end, if I know Christabel. She will be out in the kitchen, stomping her feet, and trying to talk, and asking for the steak platter. What is more, she will get it, too.

More Weegees

If anyone should ask us in a question game "Where does President Hoover get his Norwegian elkhounds?" we could answer. In fact we have met the man who gets President Hoover his elkhounds, a gentleman who, we are proud to say, is a resident of this city. There's a story about the Hoover elkhound man, too, as follows: Weegee—that's Mr. Hoover's first elkhound—so endeared himself to the president and his staff that a few weeks ago it was decided to get two more elkhounds, pups. The White House, after some fruitless scouting around in which it found that pedigreed elkhounds don't grow on trees, bethought itself of the New York authority who had obtained Weegee. We shall call him Mr. Bodley Head, that being a name we have always wanted to use. Mr. Head works for a newspaper but was at home resting when the White House phoned his office. His office called him. "Yeh?" said Mr. Head. "This is the office," said the office. "The White House is calling you and we want to know if it's all right to give them your home phone number."

JULY 30, 1932

Actor

A certain lady who saw *The Barretts of Wimpole Street* one evening lately was just as interested in the little dog that has a part in the show as she was in the performance itself, maybe more. It was her good fortune that, after the play, she encountered a chauffeur putting the dog into an automobile. She boldly went up and stroked the little fellow. "What keeps him so quiet in the show?" she asked the man. He eyed her gravely and said: "That's the part he plays, lady."

AUGUST 8, 1931

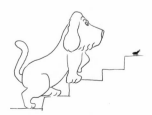

In Defense of Dogs, Even, After a Fashion, Jeannie

While digging up, for this rambling treatise, some fugitive things I had written about dogs but never preserved, I turned an old lost corner one day and came upon two ancient and conflicting pieces of indignation. One of these was a woozily implemented attack on dogs, written by Stanley Walker twenty years ago for a now dead magazine called *For Men*, and the other was a singularly persuasive and curiously moving defense of dogs, written, for a subsequent issue of the same magazine, by me. I take that last part back. I should like to be able to report that I was a skillful controversialist in those vital years, with a deceptively ingratiating courtroom manner, apt quotations from Shelley and the Bible at my fingertips, and a faint, fleeting smile playing about the corners of my inscrutable mouth, but the truth is that time has tarnished and diminished what my learned opponent and I had to say. We both used unfair tactics, pure guesswork, and what still has the ring of downright prevarication. I trust that our readers forgave us our hot-blooded impetuosity, if we had any readers. I never heard from one.

My gifted colleague's strategy consisted mainly of adducing dubious evidence of the tendency of dogs to break up the emotional relationships of men and women. He cited the case of a standard poodle that a gentleman caller filled full of brandy while his girl friend, the dog's owner, was upstairs dressing. When she finally descended, her eyes flashed lightning, for hell hath no fury like that of a lady whose dog has been debauched, and she threw her suitor out of her house and her life. The strangest exhibit offered in evidence by the prosecution, with dazzling dexterity, was the story of another gentleman caller who sat down on his sweetheart's dog, ruining the evening, frightening the neighbors, killing the dog, and terminating the love affair. Mr. Walker, with devilish cunning, suggested to the jury that the late dog was solely responsible for its own death and for the end of the affair.

I have no desire to revive the whole yellowing record of our forgotten debate, for I feel that oblivion has mercifully descended upon the back files of *For Men*, but I should like to freshen and repeat my reply to one of Mr. Walker's old indictments. "The history of the dog," he said without batting an eye, "is one of greed, double-crossing, and unspeakable lechery." I submitted then, and I resubmit, that if you stopped ten persons

on the street and asked them, "The history of what species is one of greed, double-crossing, and unspeakable lechery," six would promptly reply, "Man," three would walk on hastily without a word, and one would call the police. (Two or more would probably call the police nowadays, but the point is unimportant.)

My inherent fairness and open mind led me to admit that some dogs have been known to let people down, or stand them up, or exasperate and even distress them by unpredictable behavior. I even went so far as to confess that some of my own dogs had double-crossed me for a total, as I put it then, of sixteen or eighteen times, but I quickly added that the basic fault was, in almost every instance, my own. There were, for special examples, certain unhelpful activities of Jeannie, the Scotch terrier I owned from 1926 to 1933.

In a 1936 piece called "The Admiral on the Wheel," I recalled what Jeannie had done to me one day ten years before: "When the colored maid stepped on my glasses the other morning, it was the first time they had been broken since the late Thomas A. Edison's seventy-ninth birthday. I remember that day well, because I was working for a newspaper then and I had been

Some of my own dogs had double-crossed me for a total, as I put it then, of sixteen or eighteen times, but I quickly added that the basic fault was, in almost every instance, my own.

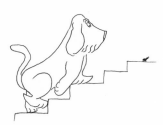

assigned to go over to West Orange that morning and interview Mr. Edison. I got up early, and, in reaching for my glasses under the bed (where I always put them), I found that Jeannie was quietly chewing them. Both tortoise-shell temples (the pieces that go over your ears) had been eaten and Jeannie was toying with the lenses in a sort of jaded way." Under the bed is no place for glasses. If I had put them on the dresser, Jeannie would never have eaten them, mainly, of course, because she couldn't reach that high, but that is beside the point.

It was neither Jeannie's fault nor mine that she embarrassed me beyond measure, about a year later, at the corner of Fifth Avenue and Eleventh Street, where she gave birth to the unexpected fifth and last of her first litter of puppies. She had begun having the pups at the ungodly hour of six A.M., in a shoe closet. It was a narrow and dark and cluttered closet, and only a female in love with chaos, or on her way back to the womb of confusion, would have selected such a place. She seemed to know less about having puppies than I did—but that is a story which would interest only a veterinarian. It was nearly three hours later, or just when the city was going to work, that the fifth pup made her appearance. I had been taking the mother dog for a walk, which both of us needed. I had a headache as the result of having had too much to drink the night before and not enough sleep. Quite a crowd gathered, which did not seem to bother Jeannie, but it bothered me. I put the newcomer in my pocket, told the loudly protesting mother to shut up, and hurried home, which was mercifully less than a block away, at 65 West Eleventh. This, as I have admitted, was neither Jeannie's fault nor mine, but the case of the large portion of apple cake was as much my fault as the glasses under the bed.

Josephine had an extraordinary fondness for Jeannie and her five pups, and her affection blandly survived the night, two months later, when the dining room became flooded with several inches of river water, a nocturnal disaster that the pups turned into a carnival. Josephine was finally aroused by a strange clatter belowstairs. She went down to discover the puppies having a wonderful time. They were not only splashing about in the water, but they had managed to launch various craft and were jumping in and out of a wooden salad bowl and other objects they had dragged into the water. Josephine later described the scene, in English, like this: "Dey laugh! Dey cry! Dey sing! Dey so happy!" Jeannie was bored by the water festival, and was lying on a broad window sill, licking her wet feet. I do not blame this night's happenings on her or anybody else, but she was certainly to blame for what happened when I took her to Columbus, Ohio, one summer on vacation.

Jeannie disappeared one morning from the home of friends my wife and I were visiting. Two days later I reported the disappearance to my old friend Harry E. French, then chief of the Columbus police department, and he assigned two detectives, whom I shall call Burke and Scanlon, to the case. I can't remember now who suggested the theory that foul play, or petty larceny, might be involved. It couldn't have been me, because I knew that Jeannie was a strayer, and it was getting harder and harder for me to conceive of anybody deliberately wanting to own her. Anyway, the detectives took over, but they let me ride with them in a squad car to the home of an ancient white-haired colored man whose seventeen children and fifty-six grandchildren were said by the detectives to be responsible for various disappearances in Columbus, of both the sentient and the insentient. It seemed that one of the grandsons

collected refuse in the neighborhood of my host and hostess. The detectives ransacked the old man's house, and appeared to be familiar with every room and every nook and cranny. The old man did not rise from his rocking chair, but kept beating on the floor with his cane and shouting, "Heah! Heah! Heah!" There was something ritualistic about the whole thing. I found myself taking sides suddenly, as if I were assuming a role in a municipal pageant. I liked the old man, and began finding fault with the methods of Burke and Scanlon, and rearranging things they had disarranged. They were monosyllabic, gum-chewing detectives and didn't seem to be on anybody's side, even each other's.

"There isn't any Scottie here," I announced finally, as they stared at me without interest, chewing slowly. "If the dog does show up," I heard myself blurt out to the old man, "you can have it."

He banged his cane and hollered, "No, no, no!" Burke and Scanlon watched us both, not narrowly, just watched, for a few moments; then they shrugged in unison and went away.

I found Jeannie two days later, through an ad in the Columbus *Dispatch*. She was staying with some people a few

houses down the block from us and they brought her home. "She acted as if she didn't belong to anybody," said the husband.

"She seemed lost and dazed," said his wife.

Before they left I put a five-dollar bill in an envelope and sealed it, and asked them if they would mind seeing that it got to their refuse collector's grandfather. They stared at me with considerably more interest than Burke and Scanlon had shown at any time, and said they certainly would, and backed away and went home.

Jeannie, as I have mentioned, was a strayer, and I once wrote a monograph about her wanderings, with some reference to the subject of roving dogs in general. I have exhumed that monograph, and it follows hereinafter, for the information and guidance of such readers as have not already had enough of Jeannieana.

Look Homeward, Jeannie

The moot and momentous question as to whether lost dogs have the mysterious power of being able to get back home from distant places over strange terrain has been argued for years by dog owners, dog haters, and other persons who really do not know much about the matter. Mr. Bergen Evans in his book, *The Natural History of Nonsense*, flatly sides with the cynics who believe that the lost dog doesn't have any more idea where he is than a babe in the woods. "Like pigeons," wrote Mr. Evans, "dogs are thought to have a super-natural ability to find their way home across hundreds, even thousands, of miles of strange terrain. The newspapers are full of stories of dogs who have miraculously turned up at the doorsteps of baffled masters who had abandoned them afar. Against these stories, however, can be set the lost and found columns of the same papers, which in almost every issue carry offers of rewards for the recovery of dogs that, apparently, couldn't find their way back from the next block." Mr. Evans, you see, touches on this difficult and absorbing subject in the uneasy manner of a minister caught alone in a parlor with an irritable schnauzer.

Now I don't actually know any more than Mr. Evans does about the dogs that are supposed to return from strange, distant places as surely as an Indian scout or a locomotive engineer, but I am not prepared to write them off as fantasy on the strength of armchair argument. Skepticism is a useful tool of the inquisitive mind, but it is scarcely a method of investigation. I would like to see an expert reporter, like Alva Johnston or Meyer Berger, set out on the trail of the homing dog and see what he would find.

I happen to have a few haphazard clippings on the fascinating subject but they are unsupported, as always, by convincing proof of any kind. The most interesting case is that of Bosco, a small dog who is reported to have returned to his house in Knoxville, Tennessee, in the winter of 1944 from Glendale, California, thus setting what is probably the world's distance record for the event, twenty-three hundred miles in seven months. His story is recorded in a book called *Just a Mutt*, by Eldon Roark, a columnist on the *Memphis Press-Scimitar*. Mr. Roark says he got his tip on the story from Bert Vincent of the *Knoxville News-Sentinel*, but in a letter to me Mr. Vincent says he has some doubts of the truth of the long trek through towns and cities and over rivers and deserts.

The dog belonged to a family named Flanigan and Mr. Vincent does not question the sincerity of their belief that the dog who turned up on their porch one day was, in fact, Bosco come home. The dog bore no collar or license, however, and identification had to be made on the tricky basis of markings and behavior. The long-distance record of Bosco must be reluctantly set down as a case that would stand up only in a court of lore.

Far-traveling dogs have become so common that jaded editors are inclined to turn their activities over to the society editors, and we may expect before long to encounter such items as this: "Rex, a bull terrier, owned by Mr. and Mrs. Charles L. Thompson of this city, returned to his home at 2334 Maybury Avenue yesterday, after a four months' trip from Florida where he was lost last February. Mr. and Mrs. Thompson's daughter,

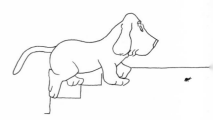

Alice Louise, is expected home tomorrow from Shipley, to spend the summer vacation."

Incidentally, and just for the sake of a fair record, my two most recent clippings on the Long Trek deal with cats, as follows: Kit-Kat, Lake Tahoe to Long Beach, California, 525 miles; Mr. Black, Stamford, Connecticut, to Atlanta, Georgia, 1,000 miles.

The homing dog reached apotheosis a few years ago when *Lassie Come Home* portrayed a collie returning to its young master over miles of wild and unfamiliar terrain in darkness and in storm. This million-dollar testament of faith, a kind of unconscious memorial to the late Albert Payson Terhune, may possibly be what inspired Bergen Evans's slighting remarks.

I suspect that Professor Evans has not owned a dog since Brownie was run over by the Chalmerses. In the presence of the "lost" dog in the next block, he is clearly on insecure ground. He assumes that the dog does not come back from the next block because it can't find its way. If this reasoning were applied to the thousands of men who disappear from their homes every year, it would exonerate them of every flaw except disorientation, and this is too facile an explanation for man or beast. Prince, the dog, has just as many reasons for getting and staying the hell out as George, the husband: an attractive female, merry companions, change of routine, words of praise, small attentions, new horizons, an easing of discipline. The dog that does not come home is too large a field of research for one investigator, and so I will confine myself to the case history of Jeannie.

Jeannie was a small Scottish terrier whose nature and behavior I observed closely over a period of years. She had no show points to speak of. Her jaw was skimpy, her haunches frail, her forelegs slightly bowed. She thought dimly and her coordination was only fair. Even in repose she had the strained, uncomfortable appearance of a woman on a bicycle.

Jeannie adjusted slowly and reluctantly to everything, including weather. Rain was a hand raised against her personally, snow a portent of evil, thunder the end of the world. She sniffed even the balmiest breeze with an air of apprehension, as if it warned of the approach of a monster at least as large as a bus.

Jeannie did everything the hard way, digging with one paw at a time, shoving out of screen doors sideways, delivering pups on the floor of a closet completely covered with shoes. When she

was six months old, she tried to bury a bone in the second section of the *New York Times*, pushing confidently and futilely at the newsprint with her muzzle. She developed a persistent troubled frown which gave her the expression of someone who is trying to repair a watch with his gloves on.

Jeannie spent the first two years of her life in the city, where her outdoor experiences were confined to trips around the block. When she was taken to the country to live, she clung to the hearth for several weeks, poking her nose out now and then for a dismaying glimpse of what she conceived to be God's great Scottie trap. The scent of lawn moles and the scurry of squirrels brought her out into the yard finally for tentative explorations, but it was a long time before she followed the woodchuck's trail up to the edge of the woods.

Within a few months Jeannie took to leaving the house when the sun came up and returning when it began to get dark. Her outings seemed to be good for her. She began to look sleek, fat, smug, and at the same time pleasantly puzzled, like a woman who finds more money in her handbag than she thought was there. I decided to follow her discreetly one day, and she led me a difficult four-mile chase to where a large group of summer people occupied a row of cottages near a lake. Jeannie, it came out, was the camp mascot. She had muzzled in, and for some time had been spending her days shaking down the cottagers for hamburgers, fried potatoes, cake, and marshmallows. They wondered where the cute little dog came from in the morning and where she went at night.

Jeannie had won them over with her only trick. She could sit up, not easily, but with amusing effort, placing her right forefoot on a log or stone, and pushing. Her sitting-up stance was teetery and precarious, but if she fell over on her back or side, she was rewarded just the same, if not, indeed, even more bountifully. She couldn't lose. The camp was a pushover.

Little old One Trick had a slow mind, but she gradually figured out that the long trip home after her orgies was a waste of time, an unnecessary loop in her new economy. Oh, she knew the way back all right, Evans—by what improbable system of landmarks I could never guess—but when she got home there was no payoff except a plain wholesome meal once a day. That was all right for young dogs and very old dogs and spaniels, but not for a terrier who had struck it rich over the hills. She took to

When she was six months old, she tried to bury a bone in the second section of the New York Times, *pushing confidently and futilely at the newsprint with her muzzle. She developed a persistent troubled frown which gave her the expression of someone who is trying to repair a watch with his gloves on.*

staying away for days at a time. I would have to go and get her in the car and bring her back.

One day, the summer people, out for a hike, brought her home themselves, and Jeannie realized the game was up, for the campers obviously believed in what was, to her, the outworn principle of legal ownership. To her dismay they showed themselves to be believers in one-man loyalty, a virtue which Jeannie had outgrown. The next time I drove to the camp to get her she wasn't there. I found out finally from the man who delivered the mail where she was. "Your little dog is on the other side of the lake," he said. "She's stayin' with a schoolteacher in a cottage the other side of the lake." I found her easily enough.

The schoolteacher, I learned, had opened her door one morning to discover a small Scottie sitting up in the front yard, begging. The cute little visitor had proceeded to take her new hostess for three meals a day, topped off now and then with chocolates. But I had located her hiding place, and the next time she disappeared from home she moved on to fresh fields. "Your little dog's stayin' with some folks over near Danbury," the mailman told me a week later. He explained how to get to the house.

"The hell with it," I said, but a few hours later I got in the car and went after her, anyway.

She was lying on the front porch of her current home in a posture of truculent possession. When I stopped the car at the curb she charged vociferously down the steps, not to greet the master, but to challenge a trespasser. When she got close enough

to recognize me, her belligerence sagged. "Better luck next time," I said, coldly. I opened the door and she climbed slowly into the car and up onto the seat beside me. We both stared straight ahead all the way home.

Jeannie was a lost dog, lost in another way than Evans understands. There wasn't anything to do about it. After all, I had my own life to live. Before long I would have had to follow her as far as Stamford or Darien or wherever the gravy happened to be thickest and the clover sweetest. "Your little dog—" the mailman began a few days later. "I know," I said "thanks," and went back into the house. She came home of her own accord about three weeks later and I think she actually made an effort to adjust herself to her real home. It was too late, though.

When Jeannie died, at the age of nine, possibly of a surfeit of Page & Shaw's, I got a very nice letter from the people she was living with at the time.

Exclusive

Hampered considerably by her Scotch terrier, Timber, who hadn't been in town for quite a while and wanted to examine everything he came to, a Boston woman finally reached a midtown kennel. She told an attendant there she wanted to board the dog for a couple of days. He told her they didn't board dogs by the day but that there was a very nice place on 196th Street. That was too, too far to go, so she took Timber over to the Waldorf, registered there, and turned the problem of boarding the dog over to the head porter. Two days later, Timber was brought back, looking well groomed and bright-eyed. The lady was surprised to find that the man who brought the dog back to her was the very kennel attendant who had refused her two days before. He remembered her, too. "You see, Madam," he explained, "we only take Waldorf dogs."

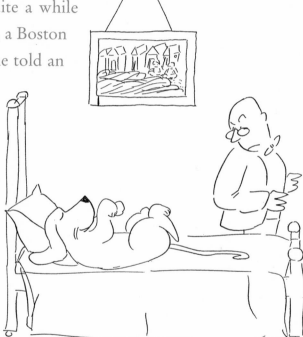

An abandoned expectant position which the masseur tried to ignore.

APRIL 14, 1934

Dog Show

"You don't understand. The mascot isn't
supposed to participate in the game."

"*Will you be good enough to dance this outside?*"

"For Heaven's sake, why don't you
go outdoors and trace something?"

"The father belonged to some people who
were driving through in a Packard."

"You're a low-down human being."

"*That's right, now try to win* him *away from me.*"

Gift

T hey are talking at Bloomingdale's (the store, not the sanitarium) about a lady who came in there leading a smart-looking little dog and asked to see books about dogs. A saleslady collected quite a pile for her, large and small, illustrated with everything from photographs to etchings of dogs. The lady opened each book, one at a time, and leaned down and showed them to Peepo—that's what she called her dog, Peepo. Peepo sniffed at the various books, at one particularly, probably because the paper and print had an interesting smell. In this one the lady promptly wrote, "To Bruno from Peepo," and asked that it be nicely wrapped up. Bruno is a dog that Peepo knows and holds in high regard and thought he ought to do something for. Or maybe Bruno is sick in bed. He sounds as if he might be.

MARCH 19, 1932

Lo, Hear the Gentle Bloodhound!

If bloodhounds could write—all that these wonderful dogs can really do, and it's plenty, is trail lost children and old ladies, and track down lawbreakers and lunatics—they would surely be able to set down more demonstrable truths about themselves than Man has discovered in several centuries of speculation and guesswork, lighted only here and there with genuine research. Books about the St. Bernard, storied angel of the mountain snows, and the German shepherd and other breeds famous for their work as army scouts, city cops, and seeing-eye dogs, sprawl all over the library, but the literature of the English bloodhound, an even greater benefactor of mankind, is meager and sketchy. Only one standard book is available, *Bloodhounds and How to Train Them*, by Dr. Leon F. Whitney of New Haven, first published in 1947 and brought out in a revised edition a few months ago.

Man doesn't even know for sure how the bloodhound got his name. Dr. Whitney, veterinarian, geneticist, and researcher, and many other authorities, subscribe to the respectable theory that the "blood" is short for "blooded," meaning a patrician, an aristocrat, a thoroughbred. My own theory is that the "blood" got into the name because of the ancient English superstition that giants and other monsters, including the hound with the Gothic head and the miraculously acute nose, could smell the blood of their prey. The giant that roared, "I smell the blood of an Englishman!" had the obscene legendary power, in my opinion, to smell blood through clothing and flesh. Nobody knows to this day the source, nature, or chemistry of the aura that sets off each human being from all others in the sensitive nostrils of every type of scent-hound, but we will get around to that profound mystery further along on this trail. It seems to me, however, that legend and lore are more likely than early breeders and fanciers to have given the bloodhound his name. In any case, it has always had a fearsome sound to the ignorant ear, and one of the gentlest of all species, probably, indeed, the gentlest, has been more maligned through the centuries than any other great Englishman with the exception of King Richard the Third.

Dictionaries, encyclopedias, and other imposing reference volumes approach the bloodhound with an air of gingerly insecurity. *Webster's International,* touching lightly on the subject, observes, truly enough, that the bloodhound was originally used

for hunting game, and adds "especially wounded game." This phrase may have grown out of the imperishable legend of blood scent, but it is also based on the fact that bloodhounds were ever slow and ponderous pursuers, more apt to catch up with a wounded stag or a stricken hart than one of unimpaired fleetness. The staid *Encyclopædia Britannica* gives our hero scant attention and alludes vaguely to an Italian type of the third century, a scent-hound, without doubt, but not a genuine bloodhound. There were scent-hounds, Dr. Whitney's researches prove, as far back as the age of Xenophon in Greece. Incidentally, the dogs that hunt by sight instead of smell, eminently the swift greyhound, originated, according to Webster, as long ago as 1300 B.C.

The sight-hounds have enjoyed, through the ages, a romantic tradition, for it is this type of canine hunter that has immemorially appeared in fairy tales, leading the mounted king and his three sons in swift pursuit of the fleet deer, which turns out in the end to be an enchanted princess. But the scent-hounds of fiction have usually been terrifying creatures, and they have done their share in bringing libel to the fair name of the bloodhound. The terrible phosphorescent Hound of the Baskervilles, which terrorized the moors and bedeviled Sherlock Holmes and Dr. Watson, was a purebred Conan Doyle hound, but if you ask the average person to identify it, he will almost always say that it was a bloodhound, as savage as all the rest of the breed. Let us sniff a little further along the trail of reference volumes, before setting out on the ancient spoor of the bloodhound itself. The austere *Oxford English Dictionary* doesn't even attempt to account for the bloodhound's name, but with its famous bloodhound ability to track down sources, comes up with these variants of the name, used in England from 1350 through the eighteenth century: "blod-hounde, bloode hownde, blude hunde, blood hunde, bloud-hound, blod-honde." The name was spelled the way it is today by Oliver Goldsmith, Sir Walter Scott, John Keats ("The wakeful bloodhound rose, and shook his hide"), and Lord Byron, who once wrote, "To have set the bloodhound mob on their patrician prey." Here the great hunter is no longer a patrician himself, but he hunts only patricians, as the Belvedere foxhounds, drawn years ago by D. T. Carlisle for *The Sportsman*, hunted only silver fox. The *O.E.D.*, by the way, adds "stolen cattle" to the bloodhound's ancient quarry of wounded stags,

wanted criminals, and wandering children. It could have brought the record up to date by putting lost dogs in the list, and at least one cat, which disappeared in an Eastern town not long ago and was found by a bloodhound that had sniffed its sandbox and followed the feline trail faithfully but with ponderous embarrassment, I feel sure.

The first scent-hound, or expert private nose, that stands out clearly in the tapestry of time is the St. Hubert of France, in the eighth century. Some of these castle-and-monastery hounds, after 1066, were imported into England, and from them sprang three English types, the talbot, the staghound, and the bloodhound. Of these, only the bloodhound remains extant. The infamous libel that clings to his name, the legend that he is a dog of awful ferocity began, in this country, before the Civil War, when foxhounds and mongrels were used to hunt down escaped slaves and were trained to fierceness. There may have been a few purebred English bloodhounds in Virginia and other southern states a hundred years ago, but the dogs that pursued Eliza across the ice in *Uncle Tom's Cabin* were crossbred, bar-sinister hounds. It was such beasts that tracked down members of James Andrew's

Northern Raiders after they had stolen the famous Iron Horse locomotive at Big Shanty, Georgia, and finally took to the woods of the Southern Confederacy. These inferior pursuers could be bought for five dollars a pair, but the purebred bloodhound then cost fifty dollars a pair. The reputation of the mongrels for ferocity was calculated to deter slaves from making a break for freedom, for if they did and were caught by the dogs, they were sometimes mangled or killed. The trail of a fugitive slave was usually fresh, and any nose-hound could follow it easily. This is also true of the trails of prisoners who escape from prison farms and penitentiaries today, and therefore the so-called "penitentiary hounds" do not need the educated nostrils of a thoroughbred. They are also trained to fierceness, since they must often deal with dangerous criminals.

However the "blood" may have got into our hero's name, it has helped to stain him almost indelibly as a cruel and feral monster. The miraculous finder of lost boys and girls, the brilliant fingerman of thousands of sheriffs' posses, policemen, and private trailers, could be safely trusted not to harm a babe in arms. Dr. Whitney's bloodhounds once found a three-year-old

Connecticut girl who had wandered away from her grandmother in a deep bramble of blackberry bushes. The dogs insisted on searching an almost impenetrable swampy region, but were deterred for hours by *Homo sapiens*, in uniform and out, who was positive the child could not have gone that far. When the human beings finally gave the dogs their own way, they dashed into the thicket. Half an hour later the hunting men came upon the little girl, sitting in a pool of water—she had taken off her playsuit to go for a swim. She was naked as a jaybird, but happy as a lark because of the two lovely wrinkled canine playmates she had just "found." Without the help of the hounds, she could never have been traced.

The *Oxford Dictionary*, with its characteristic erudition, reports that the bloodhound's Latin name is *Canis sanguinarius*, a name the Romans never used. Now *sanguinarius* does not mean blooded, in the sense of purebred; it means of or pertaining to blood, and, figuratively, bloody, bloodthirsty, sanguinary. The gentle, good-tempered, well-balanced bloodhound is actually about as fierce as Little Eva, and you simply cannot discover one provable instance of a bloodhound's attacking a child or an adult, including a cornered criminal. Dr. Whitney says the hounds don't even seem to know that teeth were made for biting. It is true that one bloodhound I heard about became understandably vexed when his master pulled him off a hot trail, and showed his indignation by a thunderous growl. It is unwise to frustrate a bloodhound who has not come to the end of a trail he is following, and how could this one have known that the bandit he was after had been apprehended, according to a telephone call, fifteen miles ahead?

It has been nearly twenty years since I came upon a flagrant piece of calumny about my friend the bloodhound, in a four-volume set of books called *The Outline of Science, a Plain Story Simply Told*, but my indignation is still as strong as it was then. The anonymous "expert" assigned to write about canines in these books had this to say: "There are few dogs which do not inspire affection; many crave it. But there are some which seem to repel us, like the bloodhound. True, Man has made him what he is. Terrible to look at and terrible to encounter, Man has raised him up to hunt down his fellowman." Accompanying the article was a picture of a dignified and melancholy English bloodhound,

about as terrible to look at as Abraham Lincoln, about as terrible to encounter as Jimmy Durante. It pleases me no end that this passage, in its careless use of English, accidentally indicts the human being: "Terrible to look at and terrible to encounter, Man. . . ." Even my beloved, though occasionally cockeyed, Lydekker's *New Natural History*, whose grizzly-bear expert pooh-poohs the idea that grizzly bears are dangerous (it seems they got the reputation of aggressiveness by rolling downhill toward the hunter after they were shot dead), knows better than to accuse the bloodhound of viciousness, or, at any rate, has the good sense to avoid the subject of his nature. Lydekker's bloodhound man contents himself with a detailed and fascinating physical description of the breed, which goes like this: "The most striking and characteristic feature of the bloodhound is its magnificent head, which is considerably larger and heavier in the male than in the female. While generally extremely massive, the head is remarkable for its narrowness between the ears, where it rises into a domelike prominence, terminating in a marked protuberance in the occipital region. The skin of the forehead, like that round the eyes, is thrown into a series of transverse puckers."

The Lydekker dog man alludes, in conclusion, to what he calls "a foreign strain of the bloodhound, which is lower on its legs than the English breed."

This foreigner could not possibly be the hound I have been putting into drawings for twenty-five years, because I was only six when the first American edition of Lydekker's *History* was brought out. My dog *is* lower on its legs than a standard bloodhound, although I would scarcely put it that way myself. He got his short legs by accident. I drew him for the first time on the cramped pages of a small memo pad in order to plague a busy realtor friend of mine given to writing down names and numbers while you were trying to talk to him in his office. The hound I draw has a fairly accurate pendulous ear, but his dot of an eye is vastly oversimplified, he doesn't have enough transverse puckers, and he is all wrong in the occipital region. He may not be as keen as a genuine bloodhound, but his heart is just as gentle; he does not want to hurt anybody or anything; and he loves serenity and heavy dinners, and wishes they would go on forever, like the brook.

The late Hendrik van Loon is the only man I have known well who owned a bloodhound, but he took his back to the ken-

nel where he had bought it, after trying in vain to teach it something besides the fine art of pursuit. Whenever Mr. van Loon called the dog, he once told me sorrowfully, it took its own good time finding him, although he might be no more than fifty feet away. This bloodhound never went directly to his master, but conscientiously followed his rambling trail. "He was not interested in me or where I was," said Mr. van Loon. "All he cared about was how I had got there." Mr. van Loon had made the mistake of assuming that a true bloodhound would fit as cozily into a real living room as my hound does in the drawings. It is a mistake to be sedulously avoided. "I would rather housebreak a moose," the great man told me with a sigh.

The English bloodhound has never been one of the most popular housedogs in the world, but this is not owing solely to the dark slander that has blackened his reputation. He is a large, enormously evident creature, likely to make a housewife fear for her antiques and draperies, and he is not given to frolic and parlor games. He is used to the outdoors. If you want a dog to chase a stick or a ball, or jump through a hoop, don't look at him. "Bloodhounds ain't any good unless you're lost," one little boy

He is a large, enormously evident creature, likely to make a housewife fear for her antiques and draperies, and he is not given to frolic and parlor games.

told me scornfully. It must be admitted that the cumbersome, jowly tracer of lost persons is somewhat blobbered and slubby (you have to make up words for unique creatures like the bloodhound and the bander-snatch). Compared to breeds whose members are numbered in multiple thousands, the bloodhound is a rare variety, and there may not be more than 1,500 or 2,000 of them in America. An accurate census is discouraged by some bloodhound kennels, many of which are not listed in the *American Kennel Gazette* for their own protection. Some years ago a Connecticut pack of twenty was poisoned, presumably by a friend or relative of some lawbreaker that one or two of the hounds had tracked down. The hounds are bred for two main purposes: to be exhibited at dog shows around the country, and to be trained for police work or private investigation. In 1954, at the annual Eastern Dog Club Show in Boston, a five-year-old bloodhound named Fancy Bombardier was selected as the best dog of all the breeds assembled there, for the first time in the forty-one-year history of the show. This was a rare distinction for our friend, for it was one of the infrequent times a bloodhound in this country ever went Best of Show. Not many judges

are as familiar with the show points of a bloodhound as they are with the simpler ones of other breeds. The wondrous Englishman, with his voluminous excess wrinkled flesh, his cathedral head and hooded, pink-hawed eyes, deep-set in their sockets, might seem to some judges too grotesque for prizes, but these are his marks of merit and aristocracy.

Bloodhound owners themselves disagree about bloodhound types and their comparative appeal, the orthodox school vehemently contending that the purebred hound is the favorite of dog-show galleries, the other school contending that the old patricians repel visitors and are frequently regarded as "hideous." There may yet be a well-defined feud between the two schools. Dr. Whitney, geneticist, eugenicist, and mammalogist, among other things, is one of those who approve of the so-called American-type bloodhound, whose anatomy is less exaggerated. Its "stream-lined" conformation is said to be a virtue in trailing, if not an advantage in the show ring. Some authorities believe that this American hound, if judiciously crossbred with the English type, would add a morganatic strain of sturdiness to the Grand Duke's descendants. The English dog, after centuries of pure breeding, does not have a powerful constitution and is subject to certain virus infections and a destructive stomach ailment called "bloat." (Six fine American-owned bloodhounds died of it last year.)

Many state police barracks, but far from enough, have at least one pair of trained bloodhounds. Perhaps the foremost police trainer and trailer in the East is Sergeant W. W. Horton of the state barracks at Hawthorne, New York. He began years ago as a corporal, and for nearly two decades he and his dogs have built up a great record tracking down the crooked and the vanished. They have worked in half a dozen different states, and three years ago Sergeant Horton and his partner were asked by the government of Bermuda to bring their dogs down there to hunt a criminal, notorious for his escapes from prison and his skill in hiding out. They were the first bloodhounds that most Bermudians had seen, and they were not warmly welcomed by the population because of the ancient superstitions about them. The dogs found the coral terrain of Bermuda a good scent-holder, but they were disturbed by crowds of people that followed them, like a gallery at a golf tournament. They traced their man, finally, down to the water's edge, where he had apparently

escaped from the island by ship. Sergeant Horton and his partner wore holstered .38 police pistols which astonished the Bermudians, who may keep guns in their homes but wouldn't dream of displaying one in public. "They thought we were making a movie," Sergeant Horton told me the other day. "Everybody kept looking for the cameras." (I tracked the sergeant down easily. He was handling the switchboard when I phoned.) Rusty, one of the two Hawthorne hounds that flew to Bermuda, died last winter at the unusual age of fifteen years.

The success of the dogs as trailers depends a great deal on what might be called the dogmanship of their trainers and handlers. Dr. Whitney, who has worked his own hounds with, and sometimes parallel to, the police of Connecticut, New York, and Rhode Island, has often found his man on cases in which official police dogs had failed. Expertness with a canine trailer is a knack, like a green thumb in the garden or a light hand in the kitchen, and some cops never get the hang of it. The training of a bloodhound may begin when the dog is a puppy, capable of toddling a trail only a few yards long, but a two-year-old beginner can sometimes be taught most of the tricks in six weeks; with others it may take six months. They may begin by watching a "runner" disappear from an automobile in which he has left his coat behind. The dog sniffs it carefully and sets out on the trail when the runner is lost to view. Youngsters are often used as runners, and they leave a blazed trail so that the handler can tell if the dogs get off the track. The handicap of time is slowly increased, and so is the number of runners. Eventually, five or more of them set out in single file and it is up to the bloodhound to follow the track of only one when the group scatters, the runner whose coat or cap or shoe the dog has examined with the sharpest nose in the world. He must learn to go up to a youngster whose shoe he has sniffed, paying no attention to another youngster, nearer at hand, who may be holding a piece of liver and smelling to high heaven of reward.

Bloodhounds have done more for humanity than all other canines and most men. Examples of their unique achievements would easily fill two sizable volumes, and I can only select a few at random. Let us begin with the late Madge, a bitch owned

many years ago by Dr. C. Fosgate of Oxford, New York. Madge was once called upon to trace a lost boy in a town upstate. The trail was twenty-four hours old. Madge climbed fences, wandered through yards, went down alleys, and presently asked to be let into a grocery. Inside, she trotted to a crate of oranges, then crossed over and placed both front paws on the counter. The grocer then remembered that a little boy had come in the morning before, taken an orange from the crate, and paid for it at the counter. The end of the trail was tragic: Madge came to a pier end at a river and plunged unhesitatingly into the water. The boy had been drowned there.

For more than a quarter of a century, up to October 1954, to be exact, the record for following the coldest trail, 105 hours old, was held by a male named Nick Carter, generally considered to have been the greatest bloodhound that ever lived. He was part of the most fabulous pack of bloodhounds in our history, one belonging to the late Captain Volney G. Mullikin of Kentucky. An entire volume could be devoted to the Mullikin hounds alone, and to their colorful master. From about 1897 until 1932, the Mullikin hounds brought about the capture of 2,500 criminals and wrongdoers in Kentucky, Tennessee, West Virginia, and other states. A hundred of them were wanted for murder, others for rape, or burglary, or moonshining, or sabotage (Captain Mullikin got $5,000 from a West Virginia coal company for tracking down a gang of saboteurs), and almost every other crime in the calendar, including arson. Nick Carter's old cold trail of four days and nine hours brought to justice a man who had burned down a hen house, but he closed a total of six hundred cases, most of them major, during his great career, and no other dog has ever come close to that accomplishment. The Nick Carter case that I have encountered most often in my researches was one in which he brought to justice a group of mischievous youngsters who, for many weeks, had been in the habit of throwing rocks through the windows of houses at night and easily avoiding capture by the police. Nick was finally allowed to sniff one of the rocks which had been pulled out from under a bed with a cane and placed on a newspaper. Nick got the first of the young miscreants in a matter of hours, and the other boys were soon rounded up.

Captain Mullikin, whose photograph shows a lean, rangy, keen-eyed man, was brave to the point of foolhardiness, and

more than once stood off lynching mobs, protecting a prisoner whose guilt had not been proved. He and his dogs were in the bloody midst of the Howard-Baker and Hatfield-McCoy mountain feuds, and ran to earth a number of assassins on both sides of each of these family wars. The captain's body showed scores of buckshot scars, most of them on his legs. The fame of the Kentucky pack and its valiant leader spread as far as Cuba, and the government of that island hired the Kentuckians, on a six-months' contract, to capture a notorious bandit. The hounds caught up with the man in a matter of days, but the Cuban government insisted on paying the full six months' fee agreed upon.

When Captain Mullikin died, he left much of his bloodhoundiana, including a mountain of newspaper clippings reciting the glorious feats of the captain and his dogs, to Dr. Whitney, to whose book I am indebted for these all too brief Mullikin facts. The doctor was also given the harness that had been worn by Nick Carter on his hundreds of cases. When a hound starts out on a trail, his leash is unfastened from his collar and snapped onto his harness, and this forms the go-ahead signal, along with some such invariable command as "Find him" or "Go get 'em."

Incidentally, there are two kinds of working bloodhounds, known as open trailers—the ones that bay as they go—and mute trailers—the dogs that give no sign of their approach—and you can get into a rousing argument about comparative values in this field, too. Hounds of any kind hunting by themselves, alone or in pairs or packs, always bay on the trail of an animal quarry, but the leashed bloodhound can be taught either sound or silence in trailing a human being. No bloodhound ever gives tongue when he gets off the scent, which, it should be pointed out, is by no means the mere width of a footprint, but can sometimes be picked up by the dogs over an area of a hundred feet or more.

I called one day on the eight bloodhounds owned by Thomas Sheahan, a factory worker and past president of the American Bloodhound Club, which has only seventy members and is now headed by Mrs. Clendenin J. Ryan. One of hers, Champion Rye of Panther Ledge, beat out Mr. Sheahan's Fancy Bombardier for best of breed at a show last April. Fancy and Rye had met a number of times, however, and the former holds the edge in victories. The Sheahan hounds are neighbors of mine, kenneled at Torrington, twenty miles away. The chief of the pack

is, of course, Fancy Bombardier, a couchant hound in the best tradition of austere and pensive Rodinesque posture. A grown poodle poses with the professional grace of an actress, but a bloodhound resembles a Supreme Court justice gravely submitting to the indignity of being photographed. Bloodhounds may look exactly alike to the layman, but they are not turned out of a rigid mold, like cast-iron lawn dogs. Bombardier's son, Essex Tommy, whose late grandfather had a fine trailing record with

the Bethany State Police Barracks in Connecticut, is a wag, a gay-heart, with the bloodhound habit of rearing up and planting his big friendly paws on your chest. This affable bloodhound mannerism has been known to frighten a cornered culprit, who does not realize his big pursuer merely wants to shake hands, like the American colonel who captured Hermann Goering at the end of the war.

The Sheahan hounds are bred for show, not trailing, although a few have joined the Connecticut State Police. One of the hounds kept digging solemnly deep into the ground while I was there, hunting for the roots of a tree, which all dogs love to chew. A nine-month-old female got into a loud altercation with a fourteen-year-old German shepherd—something about a missing bone—but there was no biting, only argument and accusation. As puppies, bloodhounds are almost as playful as other dogs, but they soon become sedentary and are interested in no game except professional hide-and-seek. They are brought up outdoors, to thicken their coats and toughen them, but they have to be introduced to rough weather gradually. Once acclimatized, a sound dog may be able to sleep in the snow without chill or

A grown poodle poses with the professional grace of an actress, but a bloodhound resembles a Supreme Court justice gravely submitting to the indignity of being photographed.

frostbite. They are neither climbers nor jumpers, and often have to be lifted over fences and other obstacles. Worn out after a long trail, they may have to be carried and fall asleep easily in their trainers' arms. Mr. Sheahan pulled down the lower eyelid of one patient bloodhound, to show its deep-set reddish eye, which seems to be slowly on its way to becoming vestigial. The stronger the nose, the weaker the eye, generally speaking, and bloodhounds sometimes bump into things on a trail. "You shouldn't be able to see a bloodhound's eye at a distance of thirty feet," Mr. Sheahan said. This is a show point in a true bloodhound's favor. Bloodhounds have a short vocabulary, and few changes of inflection or intonation. Fancy Bombardier kept saying "Who?" deepening the volume as his questioning went on. "*Who?*" he demanded. "Ralph!" I barked. "*Who?*" he roared. "Ralph, Ralph Rolf," I said, and so the stolid cross-examination continued.

The bloodhound is not a commercial dog, and few kennel owners break even financially. A good male puppy usually brings about a hundred dollars, rarely more than three hundred, and eight hundred to a thousand dollars is a high price nowadays for a trained adult of either sex. The first bloodhounds brought into this country from England in this century, around 1905, included some that had cost from $2,000 to $3,500. The prices got lower as the popularity of the breed slowly began to decline. It has come up sharply in recent years, but even so, only 195 new bloodhounds were registered with the American Kennel Club last year. Thomas Sheahan and another eminent bloodhound man, Clarence Fischer of Kingston, New York, recently recommended a $550 perfect male specimen to George Brooks of LaCrosse, Wisconsin, who bought the dog on their say-so without having seen it. Mr. Fischer, whom some of his colleagues call the most dedicated bloodhound man in America, if not the world, owns the finest and most extensive collection of bloodhoundiana in the country, and has known personally most of the leading American owners and trainers. George Brooks, who works in a drugstore when he is not on the trail, is considered one of the outstanding tracers. His dogs often work at night, since they are less distracted by sights and sounds, and young dogs just learning the trade do much better in the dark. The Brooks hounds specialize in city trailing, and their services are often required by police departments in the Middle West, but they can take on a country job and do just as well. Last winter they followed the tragic trail of two little boys to a hole in the ice of a river where they had drowned.

Most of the trails of lost children and adults fortunately end in the discovery of the persons alive and well. Some police authorities approve of perpetuating the libel that a bloodhound is a savage beast, accustomed to tearing his quarry to bits when he comes upon it. The purpose of this wrong-minded philosophy is to deter evil-doers, and make them think twice before committing a crime and seeking to escape. It is a badly thought-out reversion to the theory and practice of southern slaveowners a hundred years ago and, the point of morality aside, it is calculated to cause the parents of wandering children to fear the use of bloodhounds.

There is a widespread belief, among the uninitiated, that the bloodhound's usefulness in tracking down criminals came to an end with the era of the automobile and the advent of the getaway car. This is only partly true. It is common knowledge that our olfactory genius is interested in automobiles only for what they may contain in the way of human odors, and could not possibly tell a Buick from a Packard, or one tire from another.

Everybody also knows that no hound, even if it were able to follow a tire trail, could trace an automobile over hundreds or thousands of miles. But these self-evident facts by no means completely hamstring or footcuff the relentless pursuers. Many fleeing criminals abandon their cars sooner or later, usually alongside a wooded area, thus becoming a setup for bloodhounds. The dogs will get into an abandoned car, inhale a long snoutful of evidence, and set out gleefully and confidently on the track into the woods. They can tell more about the driver or other occupants of an empty motorcar than the police experts in any laboratory. And, remarkable to say, bloodhounds have been known to follow the hot, short trail of a car by picking up, some yards off the road, the scent of the fugitive, if they have previously been able to sniff some personal belonging of his. One hound trotted in a ditch, parallel to the highway, for four miles, apparently detecting with ease the scent of his quarry, car or no car. This particular fugitive had made the mistake of turning into a driveway, four miles from his point of departure, and there was the car, and there was the man, and there, finally, was the hound, ready to shake hands and be congratulated.

This is probably the point at which I should dwell, briefly and in all bewilderment, upon just what it is that human scent consists of. All anybody seems to know is that the distinctive human smell the bloodhound selects from all others must have the infinite variability of fingerprints. Only the bloodhound comprehends this scent, which is so sharp to him and so mysterious to us, and all he has ever said about it is "Who?" Some

bloodhound men think of the scent as a kind of effluvium, an invisible exudation that clings low to the earth, about the footprints of men. Whatever it may be, a few facts are definitely known about certain of its manifestations. Dampness, especially that of light rain or dew, often serves to bring out the scent, and it is further preserved by "covers" which, in the argot of the trailer, means underbrush, thicket, low-spreading plants and bushes, and the like. Bloodhounds are frequently handicapped by what is technically known as the "fouling" of a trail by sightseers and other careless humans. Wind also adds to the troubles of a hound, along with thoughtless trampling by men, in the case of a hunt over snow. One of the hounds belonging to Mr. and Mrs. Robert Noerr of Stamford, Connecticut, is now working out of Anchorage, Alaska, helping to find persons lost in the snows.

The 105-hour record for cold trailing, so long held by the celebrated Nick Carter, was shattered in October 1954 by the well-nigh-incredible achievement of three bloodhounds belonging to Norman W. Wilson of Los Gatos, California, a former navy pilot who dedicated himself to the training of bloodhounds

Only the bloodhound comprehends this scent, which is so sharp to him and so mysterious to us, and all he has ever said about it is "Who?"

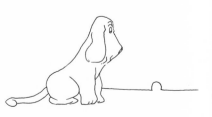

after a friend of his had become lost in the Everglades and was found by some Florida hounds. On October 9, 1954, a man and his wife and their thirteen-year-old son went deer hunting in a heavily wooded region of Oregon, thick with second-growth fir and a dense undergrowth of ferns and brush. Just a week later their car was found parked near the woods. The sheriff of the county, aided by two hundred men, an airplane and a helicopter, searched the almost impenetrable area without avail for six days. Wilson and his dogs arrived by plane, and the dogs picked up the ancient scent near the car, using as a scent guide a pair of the wife's stockings. Their leashes were fastened to their harness and the command "Find them!" was given at 9:45 on the night of October 22, 322 hours after the family was thought to have left their car. The dogs "cast" in wide circles, trying to pick up the trail, until three o'clock the next morning, and resumed the search shortly after six o'clock. There had been rains on the night of October 10 and later, and the underbrush and ferns were wet. Fifteen hours after they had taken up the search, or 337 hours after the supposed entrance of the family into the woods, one of the hounds led its trailer to the body of the youngster. The parents were subsequently found, also dead. Mr. Wilson and the sheriff and other officials later submitted the story of the remarkable search, in affidavit form, to the Blood-hound Club, and it seems likely that the amazing new record will be officially accepted. The hounds had led the human searchers in a different direction from that which the sheriff and his two hundred men had taken, in their own dogless and fruit-less search. Mr. Wilson, it should be said, receives no reward for his services and those of his hounds, beyond the expenses involved in a hunt. He had offered to help after reading about the missing persons in the newspapers. Nobody had thought to send for bloodhounds.

Curiously enough, no bloodhound man seems ever to have experimented to find out how many hours, or days, or per-haps even months or years, the scent of a man or a woman or a child might still cling to something that had once been worn. It is an obvious and interesting area of research, and I am sure the dogs would love it.

One of my favorite bloodhounds is Symbol of Ken-wood, a two-year-old from one of the excellent kennels on the

West Coast, and a member of the New Mexico Mounted Patrol. Last December, Symbol traced two men, wanted for the murder of an Albuquerque policeman, down to the edge of the Rio Grande, promptly hit the water and swam across the river and pointed out his men. They had thought the broad expanse of water would frustrate any pursuing bloodhound. Symbol's feat made up for his impish delinquency of a few days earlier, when he had dug his way out of his kennel and wandered off. He was gone for forty-eight hours, and members of the Mounted Patrol looked for him in vain. He came home, finally, in excellent spirits, having presumably backtracked his own trail. He must have had a twinkle in his grave deep-set eyes as he rejoined the tired and baffled patrol, and I hope he wasn't punished too much. Everybody probably had his own theory as to where Symbol had gone, and everybody was wrong, as Man so often is in dealing with the bloodhound breed. These patient dogs have used, many a time and oft, their one mono-syllabic interrogation in dialogue with men, who think their own wisdom is so superior. I wish I could be present some day to hear one of these man-and-dog conversations. Let us say that a parent, or a police officer, or a posse man is speaking first, like this:

"No child could possibly have got through that hedge, according to Sheriff Spencer and Police Chief MacGowan."

"Who?"

And here, gentle reader, let us leave our amazing hero, with the last, and only truly authoritative word.

No More Tricks

A kittenish hostess in her forties has a Scottie which she taught, after weeks of patient instruction, to sit up, jump over her foot, and a couple of other small tricks. At a party she gave, the dog was made to go through his repertory for each guest or group of guests that showed up. After an hour of this the dog abruptly refused to perform. The hostess scolded him, told him she was going to shut him in a dark closet for his disobedience, and then did shut him in one. After a while the last guest appeared and the dog was let out and given another chance. He looked at his mistress's large, outstretched limb—she was trying to get him to do the foot jump for Mr. Spence—sighed, turned around, and walked back into the closet.

AUGUST 15, 1931

Show him what you want him to do and he'll do it.

226

The Hound and the Gun

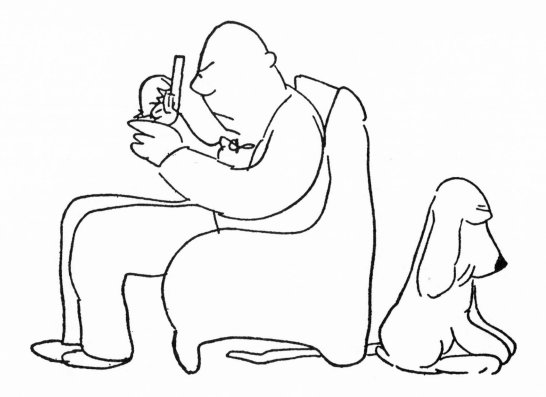

Expert

Al Smith and his colleagues are telling anecdotes of the famous old Turkish bath establishment called the Tub, which recently closed down in Albany. It was a rendezvous for notables as long ago as the eighties, when Garry Benson, a great swimmer, was its proprietor. In those days the Tub had the only swimming pool in town. One morning a society matron brought her valuable water spaniel to Garry and asked how much it would cost to teach the dog to swim. She explained she was going to spend the summer at a lake. Garry examined the dog carefully, felt its chest, tested its legs, and opined he could make an expert swimmer of the animal in eight or ten lessons, at five dollars a lesson. He did, too. When summer came and the dog was taken to the lake he plunged joyfully in, unafraid, accomplished. The lady was grateful to Mr. Benson all her life.

JUNE 22, 1929

A Glimpse of the Flatpaws

If the patient and devoted English bloodhound is a plain-clothesman, the German shepherd is a harness bull. Until six years ago, eight or more German shepherds trotted beats, each accompanied by a police officer, over in Brooklyn. The canine cops had all been presented to the Brooklyn Police Department by private citizens, but they gradually died off, or were retired, and finally no new ones appeared to take their place. They were highly proficient, perfectly trained dog cops, and they brought many a felon to justice. This squad of Brooklyn flatpaws contained one policewoman named Peggy, whose record was just as good as that of the males. I went over to Brooklyn years ago for *The New Yorker*'s "Talk of the Town" and met one of the police dogs, Nero, who was four years old at the time. We didn't shake hands. He growled low when I took a step toward him. "These dogs don't regard any man as their friend," Nero's partner, Patrolman Michael Mulcare, told me. I went back and sat down, and Nero stopped growling, but he kept his eye on me. An active, handsome, glossy animal, he wore his full equipment: collar, leash, and large leather muzzle with a broad, hard end. "They knock guys down with that muzzle," said Mulcare, "if they try to get away."

Nero walked over and sniffed me. "Hello, doggie," I said politely. Nero growled again.

"Don't move," said Mulcare. I didn't move. Mulcare commanded the dog to lie down, and he did. Then he was led away. "You can move now," said his partner.

Each dog patrolled a night beat in Flatbush with his officer. The patrolmen stayed on the streets, but, at the command "Search," the dogs went down dark alleys, into areaways, and over fences into the lawns of private houses, sniffing around for intruders. If a dog found a man—whether burglar, householder, swain throwing pebbles at a nursemaid's window, or whomever—he stood bristling beside him, growling loudly and ominously till the patrolman came up. The dog never attacked unless the man ran—or pulled a gun. If he ran, the dog dashed between his legs and tripped him, or made a flying tackle at the small of his back and knocked him down. If he pulled a gun, the dog attacked even more viciously, knocking the man down, working up to his gun hand, and, with claws and muzzle, disarming him. Gunfire merely infuriated a trained German shepherd.

The dogs practiced each day, going up ladders, climbing walls, getting into windows. Now and then at Police Department graduations—and at the Westminster Show—they put on exhibitions. They had been awarded many prizes, which were kept at the Police Academy. Once a shepherd named Rex, investigating a house closed for the season, grew suspicious of an open window on the back porch and went in to look around. When his growls and snarls brought his human partner, Rex had cornered in an upstairs room two thieves who were only too glad to surrender to a less dangerous cop.

If Brooklyn had maintained its night patrol of police dogs, they could have broken up the gang of youthful murderers that recently infested its parks and shocked the world with their meaningless killings. But the German shepherds in America have gradually been retired from police duty since the war, and are now known mainly for their work as Seeing Eye dogs. England has got far ahead of us in the use of trained shepherds to keep down nocturnal crime in the parks of its large cities. Scotland Yard has a force of more than one hundred and fifty Alsatians, and as a result of this alert patrol there were only thirteen cases of purse snatching in London's Hyde Park in 1954. In 1946, when the night watch was begun, there were eight hundred and thirty cases of purse snatching in that park.

I saw the Scotland Yard dogs in training when I was in London last June. I called at the Yard one morning and was taken out to the headquarters of the dogs in a police Humber, accompanied by Chief Superintendent John Tickle, then in charge of the flatpaws, and Chief Inspector Morgan Davies, who was about to take his turn in supervising the activities of the Alsatians. These dogs are actually German shepherds under an alias. The breed developed a reputation for ferocity in Germany even before the First World War, and the name was changed in England to free the dog from its stigma of savagery. The police dogs of Germany were trained by the use of whips and spiked collars, which tended to make them hostile to all men. The London dogs, as well as those used in Liverpool, Manchester, and Birmingham, undergo a fourteen-week course of training during which only kindness and patience are practiced by the dogs' handlers.

Unlike the shepherds of Germany and of Brooklyn, the Alsatians wear no muzzles and they are brought up in the homes

of their handlers, usually married men with children. This has made them, if not exactly affable, far less fierce than the dogs of Germany, and considerably more hospitable than the old Brooklyn squad. I found that I could move among the Alsatians without being threatened or even insulted. The thirty young dogs I watched going through their first two weeks of routine lessons kept up a constant clamor, each in its own individual tone of voice, but there was no deep growling. One dog addressed me in a low singsong, something between a bartender's snarl and the crooning of a baby. I think he was daring me to cut and run.

I was shown how the dogs go about finding a man hidden in a tree, climbing ladders and fences, and chasing and pulling to earth an "escaping criminal." Each of the dogs took its turn chasing the man who posed as the fugitive and dragging him to the ground by seizing his sleeve just above the wrist. During each of these acts, the other dogs kept up a continual whining, tugging at their leashes and begging for the signal "Get him!" This is the part of their work they like best, and they have brought down many a culprit who has tried to break away from the handlers.

One dog addressed me in a low singsong, something between a bartender's snarl and the crooning of a baby. I think he was daring me to cut and run.

The dogs have an excellent record for good behavior, on and off duty. Their work has become known far and wide; last year two London-trained Alsatians were added to the police force of Bermuda, and while I was at the training grounds, twenty miles from London, two officers from Lebanon were being schooled in the handling of shepherds. Superintendent Tickle told me, above the babel of the rookies, that the Alsatians were presented to Scotland Yard by private owners. Thirty percent of the canine candidates for the police force turn out to be unequipped for the work, because of too much pugnacity, or too much gentleness, or a downright lack of interest in climbing things or chasing people. These dogs are returned to their former masters as a rule, but some of the more aggressive ones join the Army or the Air Corps, where they are used as watch dogs for military establishments and air fields. Such installations are secure against saboteurs or night prowlers of any kind when they are guarded by a trained German shepherd.

Labradors, which were originally used, gradually disappeared from the police department because of a curious and false belief that this breed is not aggressive enough to deter criminals.

The very existence of the Alsatian patrol, on the other hand, because of the German shepherd's indelible reputation, acts as a preventive of crime in the parks of London, as it would in those of Brooklyn and other parts of New York City. Knowing this from his years of experience with the dogs, Superintendent Tickle wrote a letter to the police commissioner of New York, explaining the work of his Alsatians, but he had not received a reply after more than six months. Police officers from Germany, as well as almost every other European country, have traveled to Wickham in Kent, where the dogs are trained, to act as observers of this most famous of police-dog patrols, but New York has not yet sent any officer to Scotland Yard.

The training of a German shepherd requires as much dog-manship in its handler as the training of a bloodhound, and not every officer is fitted for the job. It may be, for all I know, that Brooklyn's postwar patrolmen turned out to lack the special knack required for working with a dog as a partner. The Brooklyn system of training was a modification of the German system, without its whips and spiked collars, and what Superintendent Tickle and his successor would like to impress upon modern police departments is the efficacy of educating the dogs in the Scotland Yard manner. The dog that lives in its handler's home is more adaptable to training than the one that sees its partner only when the night beat gets under way.

My day at Wickham began at eleven o'clock in the morning, with tea in Superintendent Tickle's office out there. I signed a handsome guest book, a gift to the Wickham Headquarters from Douglas Fairbanks, who had recently made a film called *Police Dog* with the cooperation of Scotland Yard and its Alsatians. The walls of the office were hung with photographs of some of the outstanding heroes of the dog patrol, including the only dog in the force that was ever shot at. British criminals rarely carry guns. This dog was nicked in the ear by one bullet, and three other shots went wild before he closed in on his assailant and brought him down. Even though the dogs wear no muzzles, they never mangle or maul their quarry, but simply hold him until their human partner arrives to take over. A Labrador called Big Ben, who has been with the patrol since it began, has a place of honor in the photograph gallery, since he has brought about one hundred and thirty-three arrests during

his nine-year career. Big Ben has little use for Alsatians, and, to prove that his own breed is as tough as any, if not tougher, he is always willing to take on any two Alsatians at the same time, the best day they ever saw.

Superintendent Tickle (who has recently been promoted and reassigned) is not a bloodhound man, and I was astonished to discover that he regards bloodhounds as lacking in courage. Inspector Davies had nothing to say about this theory, but I expressed my opinion one day in the London *Daily Mail*. I tried to point out that the difference between the German shepherd and the bloodhound is purely one of temperament and aptitude, like the difference between the patrolman and the plainclothes detective. I admitted that the bloodhound cannot climb ladders or fences, that it has never been known to knock anybody down except by accident, and that it would no sooner climb through an open window, looking for intruders, burly or otherwise, than I would, or my poodle Christabel. This is a matter of discretion, not a proof of cowardice, and it has kept me alive for sixty years, Christabel for fifteen, and the bloodhound breed for close to a thousand years.

I have no doubt that Big Ben could outdo a trained bloodhound in every aspect of police work except one, the successful following of an old, cold trail. The nose of the German shepherd, like that of the Labrador, has its limitations, and it must invariably give up on ancient trails that a bloodhound could take in his stride. In 1951 the Bloodhound Association of England challenged the Alsatians to a field trial, and the bloodhounds came out on top, but it was not a conclusive test because a lot of things went wrong, including some of the dogs on both sides, and their handlers. There 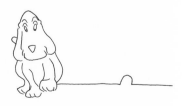 are only two bloodhound trainers left in England who were training dogs before the war, most of the other trainers having been killed in action or grown too old for this highly specialized work. The little group of devoted private owners and breeders of bloodhounds in England goes doggedly on, however, holding a field trial every year, occasionally lending its hounds to the police of a city or town here and there in the British Isles.

The great English bloodhound, in his native land, has not kept up with his American brother, but he is still on his feet, and still willing and eager to take on police-trained Alsatians over a trail from twenty-four hours to two weeks old, or even colder than that. Perhaps some day there may be an annual international field trial in which the best German shepherds and bloodhounds of the United States and Great Britain take part. I shall be glad to present a Thurber Cup to be awarded each year at this competition. And may the best bloodhound win.

Dog's Life

S cotch terriers have a way of getting into people's lives, complicating them, as into Rudyard Kipling's, who recently had to drop what he was doing and write a poem about one, and into a lady's in Connecticut who last Friday agreed to mind a friend's Scottie over the weekend. This lady, next day,

drove to town, leaving behind after considerable expostulation, Marco Polo, so-called because he wanders off a lot. Imagine her chagrin when, coming out of a grocery store, she saw Marco standing beside her automobile and realized that he had followed her after all. This was too much. She angrily seized Marco and gave him a thrashing. She did it before an interested group of onlookers. It was through one of these, in fact, that she came to realize that the dog was not Marco, but some other Scottie. She leaped into her car and drove home, leaving half her shopping undone. She now advocates that all Scotties be numbered; so does the Scottie she beat up.

MARCH 22, 1930

Beaujolais,
the Talking Poodle

W ell, what's on your mind, Bart?" Morgan pushed his cup and saucer away from him and pulled the ashtray nearer.

"If you need another advance," he said, "just say the word." A waiter pounced from nowhere and poised over the two late lunchers.

"More hot coffee, gentlemen," he said.

"Not for me," Barrett said. "I guess not, Philip," Morgan told the waiter.

"Thank you, gentlemen." The waiter disappeared.

"I could stand a brandy, Fran," Barrett said.

"Good. They got some wonderful old Armagnac here for the favorites of the maison." He hit his water glass with a spoon. "Here comes the headwaiter," he said. "The best service is none too good for us."

"What can I do for you, Mr. Morgan?" The headwaiter smiled and bowed.

"Two Armagnacs, Réné, from the secret caves. This is Mr. Barrett, Réné, Paul Barton Barrett."

"How do you do, Mr. Barrett," Réné said, bowing. Barrett nodded.

"Two Armagnacs right away, Mr. Morgan." He hurried away.

"I don't usually drink at noon," Barrett said, lighting a cigarette from one he had scarcely smoked. "Can't work if I do, but what the hell, I can't work anyway."

"Isn't the novel going well?" Morgan said. He looked worried. "I thought you said it was going fine."

"It was," Barrett said. He put out the cigarette.

"Armagnac, gentlemen," said Philip, putting two filled glasses on the table.

"What the heck's got you?" Morgan said. "Not a lady, I hope. Morgan, the big-hearted publisher, gives large advances, writes blurbs, peddles books, and what you will, but he does not advise anybody about women."

"It isn't that. It's worse than that. Good God, Fran, I'd welcome a nasty entanglement with some impossible bitch." He laughed. "That's awful funny—ironic, I mean."

"Let me in on the irony," Morgan said. Barrett fiddled with the foil of his empty cigarette pack. "You know Beau, our French poodle?"

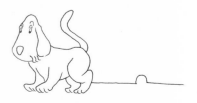

"Certainly. I suggested his name," Morgan said. "Beaujolais—Beau, for short. What's he up to—killing sheep?"

"Beau can talk," Barrett said. "He talks all the time. He can say anything you or I can say. He can hold his own in any discussion, I don't give a goddamn what it is!"

"Quiet, for Pete's sake!" Morgan said. "People are staring at you. Look, if this is a children's book you're planning, why come at it so obliquely? I'm a big boy now, with practically no sales resistance to your ideas." Barrett let out a long despondent sigh.

"I have a seven-year-old black French poodle that talks and talks brilliantly. I know that it is weird, terrible, and impossible. It is nevertheless true. You think I'm crazy, don't you?"

"Yes," Morgan said. "No." He finished his brandy. "I don't know, Bart. Why don't you go to Hot Springs for a good long rest. You've worked your tail off this summer."

"Before you have me institutionalized let me tell you exactly what happened," Barrett said.

"Sure," Morgan said. "Go ahead."

"I could stand more brandy."

"Sure," Morgan snapped his fingers, and Philip materialized. "Two more Armagnacs. Make 'em double."

"Yes sir, gentlemen." Philip melted away.

"Once a year about this time Marcia had old Admiral Mountainshed and his wife to dinner. He was a great friend of Marcia's grandfather, or maybe a great great friend of her great-grandfather."

"That's fine, old man, keep your sense of humor," Morgan said.

"Well, he used to dandle Marcia on his knee. They live only a few miles away and she can't get out of the annual dinner, or thinks she can't. The old man's mind is beginning to wander, and he's a towering bore. I wouldn't inflict him on our friends so there were just the four of us last Saturday."

"What happened?" Morgan asked.

"The old guy can't talk about anything except the Sampson-Schley controversy. He went through it at dinner, and he took it up after dinner. You think you'll go nuts. Do you want to know about Schley on the cruiser *Brooklyn* and Sampson on the battleship *New York*? I'm an expert now, naturally."

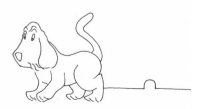

"Skip that part," Morgan said.

"He has to have a quart of milk and a glass after dinner, pours it out himself and puts pills into each glassful, dribbling on his beard and vest, which doesn't make it any easier for his audience. Beau was lying on the rug in front of the fireplace in the study, where the rest of us were having coffee. He watched the old boy with his head cocked a little on the side, as if his voice fascinated him. Mountainshed has a high wheezy voice. Suddenly he said, 'Schley was a dirty miserable cur.' You probably remember that the Navy took Sampson's side, while the public were for Schley."

"Go on," Morgan said. Philip brought their double brandies.

"At this remark, Beau opened his mouth. 'You dirty miserable human being,' he said. I'm giving it to you straight and unadorned."

"Sure." Morgan took a long drink of Armagnac. "This was in English or French?" he asked.

"English," Barrett said. "I don't know whether he speaks French or not. I suppose he does. He probably has the gift of tongues." Morgan rubbed a finger slowly around the rim of the brandy glass.

"What did the dog say?" he asked.

"He said, 'You mean a dirty miserable human being.' All right, laugh. The admiral turned to his wife. 'What's he say?' he asked, just like that. 'The dog spoke!' his wife cried. 'The dog said something.' 'What in hell and damnation did he say?' Mountainshed asked her. Marcia just sat there with her eyes popping."

"What did you do?" Morgan asked.

"I think I said, 'Quiet, Beau,' or something equally idiotic. Then the dog stood up, on all fours, I mean, and said, 'Would you let me out, Bart?' " Morgan smiled faintly.

"The worse thing about the talking dog story is it's flat," he said, "even in your skillful hands. I won't buy it. Nobody would. You know that, Bart." Barrett took a gulp of brandy.

"You're my best friend, Fran. An unusual relation between writer and publisher, but there it is. If I can't turn to you, who can I turn to?"

"Thanks," Morgan said. "I appreciate that. Go ahead. I got all day."

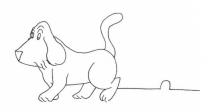

"I let the dog out," Barrett said in a low voice, "feeling the way you do when there's a nasty scene at a party and people begin to edge out, overdoing their cordial good-byes."

"You're writing it," Morgan said. "You're trying to build it up."

"Sorry," Barrett drank the last of the brandy. "Well, Mrs. Mountainshed was standing up—everybody was—when I came back. She kept saying, 'Your dog talked. That dog talked.' Mountainshed was fuming and fretting and stomping around, repeating, 'What say? What's he say?' Marcia just stood there as if she'd been hit over the head. We got rid of 'em, somehow. I don't remember much about it."

"If you'll quit twisting that tinfoil I'll get you another pack of Philip Morrises." Morgan raised his hand and the perfect waiter was there again. "What's the dog's voice like?" Morgan threw it at him suddenly as if to take him off guard.

"It's low and pleasant," Barrett said, "vibrant, too, which gives it a kind of authority, but definitely pleasant." Morgan played thoughtfully with the salt cellar. "Is it a play? Have you got a play in mind?" The waiter brought the cigarettes.

"Oh, for God's sake, Fran." Barrett made a gesture of surrender. He fussed nervously at the pack of cigarettes, trying to open it.

"Why don't I run up to Woodbury and have a chat with Beau?" Morgan grinned. "After all, we're old friends and we might turn up some mutual acquaintances, people we both knew on the Left Bank."

"I want you to come up. It'll stop your waggishness dead in his tracks." His hand shook, striking a match.

"Put yourself in my place, for God's sake, Bart," Morgan said. "I don't want to be a bad friend, but on the other hand, I don't want to be a gullible ass. Either you have a miracle in your house, of which you ought to be proud, or you are trying one of the world's corniest stories out on me. A publisher naturally doesn't want to mistake a platitude for a portent."

"You've been thinking that one up," Barrett said. "I don't say it's a portent and I don't say it's a miracle. Only a comic God would pick Marcia and me, or Mountainshed and his wife, for a revelation. There isn't a Joan or Bernadette among us. I feel sheepish about the whole thing and nervous, and a little scared,

255

but not exalted or transported. Beau has made me too mad for that, somehow, in the past week." Morgan sighed heavily.

"Take up where you got rid of the admiral and his wife. What happened then? What happened when the dog came back in the house?"

"We stood in the front hall, frightened, and bewildered and not saying anything for a while. I could see Marcia was on the verge of hysterics. 'Don't let him in! Don't let him in!' she said, finally. That wasn't good. She loves Beau and so do I. He's a fine dog, loyal intelligent, and amusing. You know poodles. They learn everything twice as fast as any other dog, including the seeing eye

training. I told her for Heaven's sake to quiet down. I told her the human being is susceptible to a lot of illusions. I opened the door and called Beau." Morgan finished his Armagnac.

"Go on," he said.

"Beau came in," Barrett went on, "talking. He said, 'I'm sorry I insulted Admiral Mountainshed; I just didn't think.' What in God's name am I going to do, Fran?"

"Well, what did you say to the dog?"

"Before I could say anything, Marcia screamed. Then she ran wildly upstairs, sobbing and crying, 'I can't stand it! I can't stand it! I can't stand it!' I took Beau into the living room." Morgan picked up the salt cellar again.

"This is beginning to get me, a little," he said.

"What do you think it's doing to me?" Barrett snapped. "The ramification, the complications are damn near insupportable. Beau has promised not to talk to the servants or to anybody in the village when he's out walking, or when they drop in. Thomas and Mildred are fine and sound a couple as you'd ever meet, but they'd leave us like a shot if that dog spoke to them. Mildred has a tricky heart and it might kill her. Beau understands

that. He's gentle and sensitive, and he seems to realize what he's got us into. But he loves to talk. So would you or I, if we were the first dog in the history of the world who could talk."

"What the hell does he talk about?" Morgan demanded.

"Everything. You bring it up, and he'll discuss it, he'll analyze it, as if he were getting at the marrow of a soup bone. It's not human reasoning or logic, of course. He's a canine intellectual. I'm just beginning to see his viewpoint. It gives you the feeling of having fallen downstairs or something. To him the human being is—well, dwarfed."

"Look," Morgan said, nervously, "look, you simply can't go on this way."

"I know that!" Barrett almost shouted.

"Now just a minute, just a minute," Morgan's voice was soothing as if he were talking to a child. "I grant the possibility that a dog might be able to talk—because of some distortion of his vocal chords, some monstrous morphological phenomenon. He might speak whole sentences, even, but like a parrot or any other talking bird, he could only repeat what he hears, meaninglessly, mindlessly."

"Any sensible, sane man would say the same thing, Fran. I would have said it myself up to last Saturday, one week ago today." He drank a whole glass of water. "Beau is neither meaningless nor mindless. He reads. He has read everything—that is everything in my library he can reach."

"Look," Morgan said, weakly.

"He has been getting books down off the shelves night after night for five years."

"Then why hasn't he spoken before?" Morgan rasped, impatiently.

"There speaks the human mind," Barrett said. "We speak before we know, we lecture before we learn, we explain before we understand." Morgan looked at him suspiciously.

"Quoting Beau?" he asked.

"Partly. He has a sharper expression though. 'Humans point the stuffed pheasant and retrieve the fallen leaf.' "

"Can he write?" Morgan asked, irritably. "If he can write I'll publish the book, with his picture on the jacket, gnawing a bone—or a human being. I could sell five billion copies." Barrett put out a cigarette and lighted another.

"I won't have him exploited. Anyway, he can't write. He could dictate, but there isn't a secretary in the world whose nerves would stand up under it. I won't have him exploited. My God, Fran, reporters and photographers would flock to my house from all over hell. Hot-dog stands would spring up, and postcard vendors. We'd go insane."

"Telephone for Mr. Barrett, gentlemen." Philip stood there with a portable phone. He plugged it in and set it in front of Barrett.

"Yeh?" Barrett said, wearily. "Oh, hello, dear. How are you? How's—Yeh. Yes. Yes, we have. Hm. Well, yes and no. I'll tell you about it. Hm? That'd be fine. Wait a minute. I'll ask him." He turned to Morgan. "Marcia wants to know if you can come up Monday for dinner and spend the night. Good. She is?" He spoke into the transmitter again. "He says fine. Beth is in Savannah. All right, darling. I'll be right up. I'm leaving from here. Good-bye, darling. Take it easy. Oh, where is he? That's good. Bye." He hung up. The hovering Philip disengaged the phone and took it away.

"Where is he?" Morgan asked.

"He went over to play with the Beckers's spaniel, Marcia says. It's always a strain for Beau, because he might absentmindedly speak to the spaniel and probably send it into a screaming fit."

"Sure," Morgan said. "I can hardly wait till Monday."

"I'll meet the 6:37," Barrett said.

"Let me split this." Morgan grabbed the check which the intuitive Philip had brought at just the right moment.

"Can't I drop you?" Barrett asked, outside the restaurant.

"Thanks. I want to walk." Barrett got into his car.

"Don't mention any of this to a soul, Fran. Promise me that."

"I won't." Morgan put an arm through the lowered window and shook hands. "Why don't you take it up with Thurber?" he asked, suddenly. "He thinks poodles are superior to human beings. It wouldn't surprise him."

"He'd blab it all over New England," Barrett said, starting the engine. "So long, Fran. See you Monday evening. Thanks for lunch and for listening." He began to drive off slowly.

"Keep your chin up!" Morgan yelled after him. He stood staring a long time after the car had turned into Fifth Avenue and disappeared from view.

Paul Barrett reached the broad straight parkway safely and unticketed, although he had given only the corner of his con-

sciousness to the changing lights, the glove and whistle, and the hurrying people. He kept going back over the short history of Beaujolais and the Barretts, in the dim, irrational hope of finding the key to the marvelous thing that had taken place in his house. It belonged to the books of Charles Fort, in the lore and legend of bleeding statures, vanishing ships, and teleported men. The Fortian wonders, though, had a romantic flair about them, and a talking poodle simply did not. A talking poodle was ludicrous and aesthetically wrong, Barrett told himself, like a human child among the apes, or like Burroughs's girl with the three blue eyes. It was funny: Three oranges, three diamonds, three birch trees—three damn near anything—were not only as pretty as, but prettier than two, because they could be arranged more attractively than the inflexible pair, but there was nothing to do with a third blue eye. "The supernatural is unnatural and unnatural is horrible," Barrett said to himself. He was still devoted to the handsome black poodle, of course, as the sensitive, the brave, the intelligent man remains devoted to a disfigured wife or child. Things could never be the same, though. The human being might be the most adjustable of animals, but there were limits to the strength of his mind and the tolerance of his emotions. The poodle had disagreed with this boast of superior powers of adaptability and accommodation. "Man has not adjusted himself to death at all, and his adjustment to life is nothing to write Homer about," the poodle had said to Barrett the previous Thursday night in the library when the servants were out. The dog had been careful to talk only when the servants were out, or not within earshot, or in bed asleep, but the strain of this tactful avoidance was considerable. "You mean home, not Homer," Barrett had told the poodle. Beau, with his amused smile, his head on one side, had said, "It would be interesting to let Homer know how little humans have changed since his day or, if you prefer, how vastly they have improved." Barrett had smoked a dozen pipes listening. "Man has not even adjusted himself to the geography of his planet, or its weather," Beau had continued. "The simplest things become to him imponderable, and ineffable. He lacks an outside intelligence to measure him fairly and truly, so that he must deepen on the distortions of self-criticism. Man's self-appraisal is usually self-praise." On the several nights he had heard the poodle out on a variety of subjects...

How to Harbor a Dog

An ingenious couple of East Fifty-sixth Street have devised a method of keeping a dog in an apartment house where it is against the rules. They had a metal tag made with the inscription, "To the Joneses from Calvin Coolidge." This they attached to their Sealyham's harness when the superintendent paid his expected visit to evict him. The dignitary referred their appeal to the agents of the building, who at once wrote the dog's owners a note suspending the anti-dog rule under the "very special circumstances."

JANUARY 21, 1928

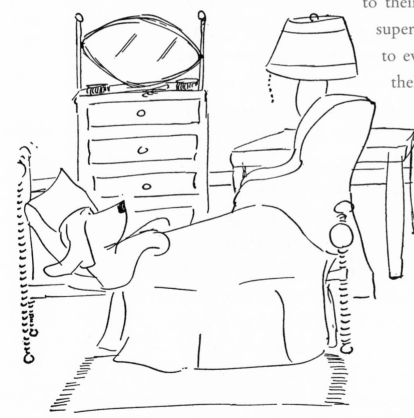

The Happier Beast

When my dog, whom I call Oliver for no particular reason, is bored with the conversation of myself and my friends, he rises from the floor and quits the room without so much as a nod. And he behaves in like manner on any and all occasions when it does not please him to remain where he is. What a boon to man would be this power simply to follow out one's secret urges!

Consider, for ready example, that particularly boring institution, the formal dinner, or banquet. How often, in the midst of endless after-dinner speech-making, does the suffering victim wish he were well out of it all, gone about his own devices! What a relief if he could but rise in his place and, like my terrier, quietly depart—not, to be sure, upon all fours, for that would be blatant and indefensible (just the departure of a canine upon his hind legs)! But simply to arise and withdraw!

If my dog does not "cotton to" the appearance or the bearing of other dogs, whether they be friends of his or strangers, he manifests his disapproval by growling. Sometimes he may even attack another dog in a direct and overt "showdown" of his feelings in the matter. It is unseemly, but who can say that it is not a physical and mental release of the utmost importance? Yet

man is denied this katharsis. He must fawn upon those friends and acquaintances who, in his heart, he would enjoy "jumping," or if he does not fawn, he must at least carry on in silence, enduring little mannerisms and habits of speech and oddities of posture which, while perhaps not intended to be annoying, nevertheless are annoying.

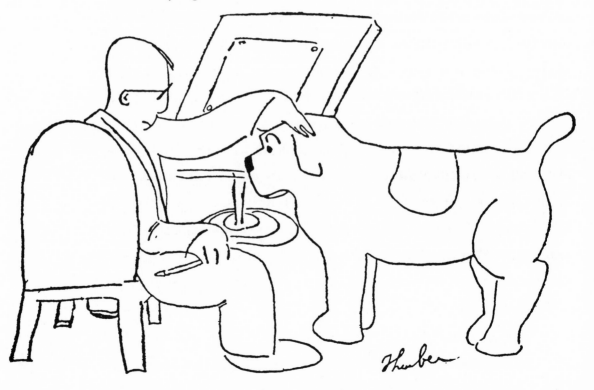

No, the dog leads a much better balanced life than man leads. Man, being a "social" creature, as opposed to an agglomeration of blissfully independent entities—which is what the dog is—finds his life shaped and rounded by those strictures which Vilfredo Pareto has called Residues and Derivations. But the only use that my Oliver could find for the great Italian scientist's ponderous *Traité de Sociologie Générale* would be to maul it about, pleasurably chewing its binding, idly destroying its (to him) meaningless and unimportant pages.

Who shall say that the animal whose brain is capable of collecting and correlating a superabundance of data on this subject and on that is, ipso facto, the superior animal? I for one shall not. I sit in my chair under a lamp and ponder the mightiest and most sonorous conclusions of our philosophers, torn by dismay and consternation and dissatisfaction. My dog lies before the fire and sleeps. One can but feel that he, of the two of us, is the happier creature.

The Hound and the Hat

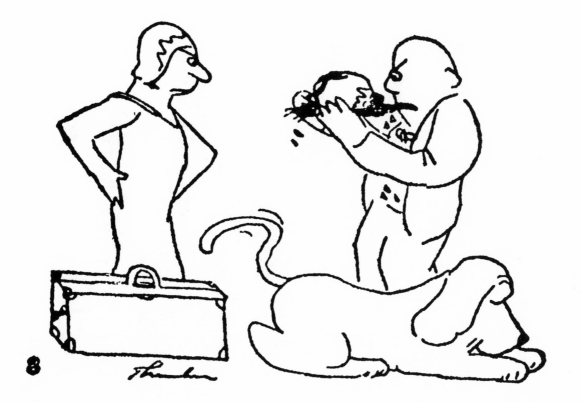

ACKNOWLEDGMENTS
AND SOURCES

For their cheerful commiseration and support, as well as for the requisite permissions to use the material included here, the editor would like to thank Sara Thurber Sauers, to whom *Thurber's Dogs* was originally dedicated, and, once again, Rosemary Thurber. My gratitude continually extends to Jay Rishel, who assisted throughout this project. Specific thanks are due to Matthew Yokom and Bruce Barnes, for creating the flip book that is derived from the original sixteen Thurber drawings, and to my agent, Doe Coover, for her generosity in bringing this new book to life.

ORIGINAL SOURCES FOR THE WRITINGS

Each entry comprises the work's original appearance in print as well as its first publication in a book by James Thurber; many pieces did not appear in book form until this volume. The author reprinted several of his most popular pieces in further compilations of his work, but present readers are to be spared further annotation.

PAGE 1: "Petting," *The New Yorker*, June 9, 1934.

3: "I Like Dogs," *For Men*, April 1939; collected for the first time in *People Have More Fun Than Anybody*, Harcourt, Brace & Company, 1994.

16: "Resourceful," *The New Yorker*, December 3, 1927.

18: "A Preface to Dogs," *The New Yorker*, January 2, 1932; collected in *Thurber's Dogs*, Simon & Schuster, 1955.

26: "Litter," *The New Yorker*, May 20, 1933.

27: "How to Name a Dog," *Good Housekeeping*, October 1944; collected in *The Beast in Me and Other Animals*, Harcourt, Brace & Company, 1948.

36: "De Luxe," *The New Yorker*, April 29, 1933.

38: From "The Pet Department," *The New Yorker*, February 22, March 1, March 15, May 3, May 17, and June 7, 1930; collected in *The Owl in the Attic and Other Perplexities*, Harper & Brothers, 1931.

47: "Don't Move," *The New Yorker*, September 19, 1936.

51: "Dogs I Have Scratched," *Harper's Bazaar*, January 1933; first collected in *People Have More Fun Than Anybody*, Harcourt, Brace & Company, 1994.

57: "Character Readings of Our Leading Canines," *Harper's Bazaar*, January 1933.

63: "The Thin Red Leash," *The New Yorker*, August 13, 1927; collected in *Thurber's Dogs*, Simon & Schuster, 1955.

76: "Hors Concours," *The New Yorker*, February 22, 1930.

78: "Canines in the Cellar," *The New Yorker*, July 28, 1951, under the title, "Lavendar with a Difference"; collected in *The Thurber Album*, Simon & Schuster, 1952.

89: "Insomnia," *The New Yorker*, April 9, 1932.

90: "A Snapshot of Rex," *The New Yorker*, March 9, 1935, under the title, "Snapshot of a Dog"; collected in *The Middle-Aged Man on the Flying Trapeze*, Harper & Brothers, 1935.

98: "The Dog That Bit People," *My Life and Hard Times*, Harper & Brothers, 1933.

111: "Little Dog," *The New Yorker*, October 13, 1934.

114: "And So to Medve," *Thurber's Dogs*, Simon & Schuster, 1955.

131: "Memorial," *PM*, October 17, 1940, in Thurber's column, "If You Ask Me"; collected in *My World and Welcome to It*, Harcourt, Brace & Company, 1942.

135: "Lady with Dog," *The New Yorker*, November 1, 1930.

144: "Christabel: Part One," *The Bermudian*, December 1950, under the title, "My Friend, the Poodle"; expanded for *Thurber's Dogs*, Simon & Schuster, 1955.

151: "As You Were," *The New Yorker*, December 15, 1934.

152: "Christabel: Part Two," *The Bermudian*, December 1950, under the title, "My Friend, the Poodle"; expanded for *Thurber's Dogs*, Simon & Schuster, 1955.

163: "More Weegees," *The New Yorker*, December 15, 1934.

166: "In Defense of Dogs, Even, After a Fashion, Jeannie," *Thurber's Dogs*, Simon & Schuster, 1955.

175: "Look Homeward, Jeannie," *New York Times Magazine*, February 8, 1948, under the title, "Notes on Talking and Homing Dogs"; collected in *The Beast in Me and Other Animals*, Harcourt, Brace & Company, 1948.

185: "Exclusive," *The New Yorker*, April 14, 1934.

193: "Gift," *The New Yorker*, March 19, 1932.

194: "Lo, Hear the Gentle Bloodhound!," *Thurber's Dogs*, Simon & Schuster, 1955.

226: "No More Tricks," *The New Yorker*, August 15, 1931.

233: "Expert," *The New Yorker*, June 22, 1929.

234: "A Glimpse of the Flatpaws," *Thurber's Dogs*, Simon & Schuster, 1955.

245: "Dog's Life," *The New Yorker*, March 22, 1930.

247: "Beaujolais, the Talking Poodle," unpublished.

264: "How to Harbor a Dog," *The New Yorker*, January 21, 1928.

265: "The Happier Beast," *The New Yorker*, January 13, 1934. Originally signed "Rags," this was part of the *Punch* parody issue.

ORIGINAL SOURCES FOR THE DRAWINGS

With the exception of those drawings Thurber originally created to accompany specific texts, such as the illustrations for "The Pet Department," the drawings selected throughout the book come from various magazines and books, and are listed here. The "flip book" that runs at the lower-right-hand corner of this book is derived from sixteen drawings, "The Hound and the Bug," which initially appeared in *The Seal in the Bedroom*, Harper & Brothers, 1932. Since Thurber often used his drawings in several books, and, particularly after his eyesight prevented him from creating new drawings, applied previously created illustration to new texts, book annotations are not given for the following illustrations except when a drawing appears for the first time in a posthumously published volume.

Photographs appear courtesy of Rosemary Thurber and the estate of James Thurber.

COVER ILLUSTRATION: [Man on all fours, face-to-face with dog] *The Owl in the Attic and Other Perplexities*, Harper & Brothers, 1931.

COVER PHOTOGRAPH: Thurber with his poodle, Christabel.

BACK COVER: [Huge dog staring down frightened man] frontispiece, *Let Your Mind Alone!*, Harper & Brothers, 1937.

HALF TITLE: [Winged, flying dog] *The New Yorker*, September 21, 1935; first collected in *People Have More Fun Than Anybody*, Harcourt, Brace & Company, 1994.

FRONTISPIECE PHOTOGRAPH: James Thurber with unidentified dog, 1936.

TITLE PAGE: [Dog at bottom of long staircase] originally appeared with the caption "Dogs suffer from depression," from *How to Raise a Dog: In the City . . . in the Suburbs*, by James R. Kinney, V.M.D., with Ann Honeycutt, Simon & Schuster, 1938.

CONTENTS: [Two dogs as bookends] *The New Yorker*, December 7, 1935.

COPYRIGHT PAGE: [Dog and woman tug-of-war] *The New Yorker*, March 29, 1941.

PAGE vi: [Framed dogs] excerpt from cartoon entitled, "I yielded, yes—but I never led your husband on, Mrs. Fisher!" *The New Yorker*, April 2, 1932.

1: "He lies down on the sidewalk when you're trying to make him heel," from *How to Raise a Dog: In the City . . . in the Suburbs*, by James R. Kinney, V.M.D., with Ann Honeycutt, Simon & Schuster, 1938.

2: [Fourteen different dogs] detail from cover, *The New Yorker*, February 9, 1936.

6: [Man spoon-feeding dog], originally appeared with the caption "Hand-feeding is one of the commonest solutions," from *How to Raise a Dog: In the City . . . in the Suburbs*, by James R. Kinney, V.M.D., with Ann Honeycutt, Simon & Schuster, 1938.

8: [Pair of dogs, looking up] *The New Yorker*, March 14, 1942; first collected in *People Have More Fun Than Anybody*, Harcourt, Brace & Company, 1994.

17: [Dog peering out door in snow] *The New Yorker*, January 5, 1935.

18: "If it can be said that life in any household with any puppy can ever be called a rut," from *How to Raise a Dog: In the City . . . in the Suburbs*, by James R. Kinney, V.M.D., with Ann Honeycutt, Simon & Schuster, 1938.

20: "At the end of six weeks she tells them to scram," from *How to Raise a Dog: In the City . . . in the Suburbs*, by James R. Kinney, V.M.D., with Ann Honeycutt, Simon & Schuster, 1938.

22: "Owners have too often fixed up fancy quarters for a prospective mother only to find that she preferred the hall closet," from *How to Raise a Dog: In the City . . . in the Suburbs*, by James R. Kinney, V.M.D., with Ann Honeycutt, Simon & Schuster, 1938.

26: "A litter of perfectly healthy puppies raised on fried pancakes," from *How to Raise a Dog: In the City . . . in the Suburbs*, by James R. Kinney, V.M.D., with Ann Honeycutt, Simon & Schuster, 1938.

29: [Hound with butterfly] *Fables for Our Time*, Harper & Brothers, 1940.

32: [Woman writing, man, dog] Cover for *The Pocket Entertainer*, Shirley Cunningham, editor, Pocket Books, 1942; first collected in *Collecting Himself: James Thurber on Writing and Writers, Humor and Himself*, Harper & Row, 1989.

37: "Dogs are getting dressier by the minute," from *How to Raise a Dog: In the City . . . in the Suburbs*, by James R. Kinney, V.M.D., with Ann Honeycutt, Simon & Schuster, 1938.

48: "Comb the woods!" *The Beast in Me and Other Animals*, Harcourt, Brace & Company, 1948.

52: [Dog looking up at man] *Williams Record*, April 13, 1940; first collected in *People Have More Fun Than Anybody*, Harcourt, Brace & Company, 1994.

54: [Resting man and dog asleep at his feet] *The New Yorker*, April 8, 1933.

63: "The dog's attitude toward love remains today exactly the same as it was in 6000 B.C.," from *How to Raise a Dog: In the City . . . in the Suburbs*, by James R. Kinney, V.M.D., with Ann Honeycutt, Simon & Schuster, 1938.

67: "Secretly they are always comparing you unfavorably with their former master," from *How to Raise a Dog: In the City . . . in the Suburbs*, by James R. Kinney, V.M.D., with Ann Honeycutt, Simon & Schuster, 1938.

68: "In time the dog world will undoubtedly have its Freuds and Jungs," from *How to Raise a Dog: In the City . . . in the Suburbs*, by James R. Kinney, V.M.D., with Ann Honeycutt, Simon & Schuster, 1938.

69: "Here's a study for you doctor—he faints." *The Seal in the Bedroom*, Harper & Brothers, 1932.

70: "Some dogs actually cry," from *How to Raise a Dog: In the City . . . in the Suburbs*, by James R. Kinney, V.M.D., with Ann Honeycutt, Simon & Schuster, 1938.

71: "A dog doesn't necessarily love the person who feeds him," from *How to Raise a Dog: In the City . . . in the Suburbs*, by James R. Kinney, V.M.D., with Ann Honeycutt, Simon & Schuster, 1938.

72: "If the owner jumps every time he hears the doorbell ring, the dog will show nervousness too," from *How to Raise a Dog: In the City . . . in the Suburbs*, by James R. Kinney, V.M.D., with Ann Honeycutt, Simon & Schuster, 1938.

73: [Woman with dog, tangled in leash of another dog] cover for *How to Raise a*

Dog: In the City . . . in the Suburbs, by James R. Kinney, V.M.D., with Ann Honeycutt, Simon & Schuster, 1938.

74: "Nor have I found that females are more intelligent than males," from *How to Raise a Dog: In the City . . . in the Suburbs*, by James R. Kinney, V.M.D., with Ann Honeycutt, Simon & Schuster, 1938.

75: "She would show him the way to the safe," from *How to Raise a Dog: In the City . . . in the Suburbs*, by James R. Kinney, V.M.D., with Ann Honeycutt, Simon & Schuster, 1938.

76: "Go away, you look human," *Waterbury* (Conn.) *Republican*, January 19, 1939; first collected in *People Have More Fun Than Anybody*, Harcourt, Brace & Company, 1994.

77: [Bon voyage with couple and their dogs] ad for French Line cruises, *The New Yorker*, May 6, 1933.

78: [Dog descending stairs, purse in mouth] *The New Yorker*, June 10, 1939.

84: [Dog toppling man and furniture], originally appeared with the caption "You need the strength and endurance of a wrestler," from *How to Raise a Dog: In the City . . . in the Suburbs*, by James R. Kinney, V.M.D., with Ann Honeycutt, Simon & Schuster, 1938.

87: Family photograph of Scotty, Thurber's grandfather's dog.

89: "Your child brings home a scraggly puppy from Lord knows where," from *How to Raise a Dog: In the City . . . in the Suburbs*, by James R. Kinney, V.M.D., with Ann Honeycutt, Simon & Schuster, 1938.

90: Family photograph of Rex, undated.

92: [Sleeping dog] *The Middle-Aged Man on the Flying Trapeze*, Harper & Brothers, 1935.

93: "Roy had to throw Rex." Originally illustrated "The Night the Bed Fell," from *My Life and Hard Times*, Harper & Brothers, 1933.

98: "Nobody knew exactly what was the matter with him," from "The Dog That Bit People," from *My Life and Hard Times*, Harper & Brothers, 1933.

105: [Dog standing on bench, forepaws on table, looking over his shoulder] originally captioned "Muggs at his meals was an unusual sight," from *My Life and Hard Times*, Harper & Brothers, 1933.

106: Family photograph of Muggs, undated.

107: "Thunderstorms have driven more than one dog into hysterics," from *How to Raise a Dog: In the City . . . in the Suburbs*, by James R. Kinney, V.M.D., with Ann Honeycutt, Simon & Schuster, 1938.

108: Family photograph of Muggs, 1920s.

110: [Man behind tree, woman running with dog], cover, *The New Yorker*, February 29, 1936. First collected *in People Have More Fun Than Anybody*, Harcourt, Brace & Company, 1994.

115: [Walking standard poodle] originally illustrated "The Monroes Find a Terminal," in *Thurber's Dogs*, Simon & Schuster, 1955.

116: [Standard poodle play-bowing] originally illustrated "The Monroes Find a Terminal," in *Thurber's Dogs*, Simon & Schuster, 1955.

119: Family photograph of Medve, undated.

125: Family photograph of Medve with Althea Thurber and daughter, Rosemary Thurber.

131: [Dog looking at grave marker] *Bermudian*, November 1950, to accompany "Ave Atque Vale." Initially Thurber had suggested using the drawing to accompany the obituary of Harold Ross in *The New Yorker*; first collected in *Collecting Himself: James Thurber on Writing and Writers, Humor and Himself*, Harper & Row, 1989.

136: [Woman carrying dog and suitcase] originally illustrated "The Departure of Emma Inch," from *The Middle-Aged Man on the Flying Trapeze*, Harper & Brothers, 1935.

137: "Shut up, Prince! What's biting you?" *The New Yorker*, April 27, 1935.

138: "Other end, Mr. Pemberton." *The New Yorker*, February 9, 1935.

139: "Mush!" *The New Yorker*, January 30, 1937.

140: [Skiing dog] *The New Yorker*, January 25, 1941; first collected in *People Have More Fun Than Anybody*, Harcourt, Brace & Company, 1994.

141: "Are you two looking for trouble, mister?" *The New Yorker*, May 19, 1934.

142: "I'm very sorry, madam, but the one in the middle is stuffed, poor fellow." *The New Yorker*, March 7, 1936.

143: "He's in love with a basset who moved away." *Thurber's Dogs*, Simon & Schuster, 1955.

144: [Dog balancing ball on nose] *Fables for Our Time*, Harper & Brothers, 1940.

145: Photograph by Coviello: James Thurber with poodle and toy "Thurber dog." *Waterbury Connecticut Republican*, 1954.

189: "For Heaven's sake, why don't you go outdoors and trace something." *The New Yorker*, March 4, 1933.

190: "The father belonged to some people who were driving through in a Packard." *The New Yorker*, June 11, 1932.

191: "You're a low-down human being." *Thurber's Dogs*, Simon & Schuster, 1955.

192: "That's right, now try to win *him* away from me." *The New Yorker*, November 13, 1943.

193: [Dog reading book] *Fables for Our Time*, Harper & Brothers, 1940.

194: [Bloodhound sniffing footprints] from "Lo, Hear the Gentle Bloodhound!" *Thurber's Dogs*, Simon & Schuster, 1955.

198: [Bloodhound pursuing man] from "Lo, Hear the Gentle Bloodhound!" *Thurber's Dogs*, Simon & Schuster, 1955.

202: [Bloodhound sniffing two footprints] originally illustrated "The Patient Bloodhound," in *Fables for Our Time*, Harper and Brothers, 1940.

208: [Bloodhound with collar] from an unpublished letter; first collected in *People Have More Fun Than Anybody*, Harcourt, Brace & Company, 1994.

214: [Dog sniffing box] *The Middle-Aged Man on the Flying Trapeze*, Harper & Brothers, 1935.

220: [Pair of dogs with turtle and frog] from *The Beast in Me and Other Animals*, Harcourt Brace & Company, 1948.

226: "Show him what you want him to do and he'll do it," from *How to Raise a Dog: In the City . . . in the Suburbs*, by James R. Kinney, V.M.D., with Ann Honeycutt, Simon & Schuster, 1938.

227: "The Hound and the Gun," *Thurber's Dogs*, Simon & Schuster, 1955.

232: [Dogs on islands] originally illustrated the word "canary" for a book of etymologies, *In a Word*, by Margaret S. Ernst, Alfred A. Knopf, 1939.

237: [Running dog] *Ladies' Home Journal*, July 1946.

240: [Two dogs challenging each other] from *The Beast in Me and Other Animals*, Harcourt Brace & Company, 1948.

243: [Rabbit chasing dog] originally illustrated the word "preposterous" for a book of etymologies, *In a Word*, by Margaret S. Ernst, Alfred A. Knopf, 1939.

245: [Dog asleep in bed, woman awake] *Thurber's Dog's*, Simon & Schuster, 1955.

248: [Man and dog heading into a café] originally appeared with the caption, "He goes with his owner into bars," from *How to Raise a Dog: In the City . . . in the*

Suburbs, by James R. Kinney, V.M.D., with Ann Honeycutt, Simon & Schuster, 1938.

252: [Dog barking into the air] title page illustration, *The Beast in Me and Other Animals*, Harcourt, Brace & Company, 1948.

256: [Dog watching writer at desk] *PM*, October 3, 1940; first collected in *Collecting Himself: James Thurber on Writing and Writers, Humor and Himself*, Harper & Row, 1989.

261: [Dog sleeping in chair] in *Fables for Our Time*, Harper and Brothers, 1940.

264: [Dog tucked into bed at home] originally appeared with the caption "The dog will be calmer at home," from *How to Raise a Dog: In the City . . . in the Suburbs*, by James R. Kinney, V.M.D., with Ann Honeycutt, Simon & Schuster, 1938.

266: [Artist with large dog] *New York Times*, March 1, 1931; first collected in *Collecting Himself: James Thurber on Writing and Writers, Humor and Himself*, Harper & Row, 1989.

267: [Dog smelling autumn leaves] *The New Yorker*, October 13, 1945; first collected in *People Have More Fun Than Anybody*, Harcourt, Brace & Company, 1994.

276: [Baby and dog with bone] *The New Yorker*, July, 2, 1938.